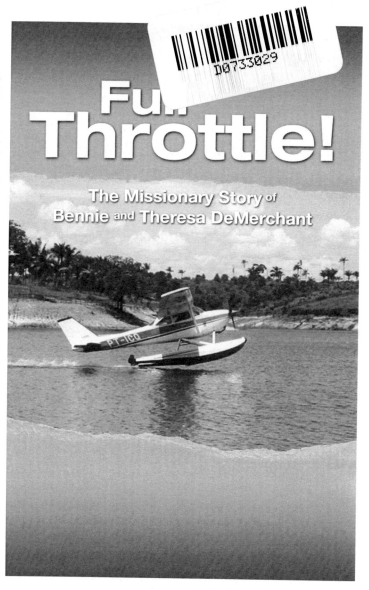

Full Throttle!

The Missionary Story of Bennie and Theresa DeMerchant

Full Throttle!

The Missionary Story of Bennie and Theresa DeMerchant

Bennie DeMerchant
Dolly McElhaney

Full Throttle!

by Bennie DeMerchant and Dolly McElhaney

WORD AFLAME PRESS
8855 Dunn Road, Hazelwood, MO 63042
www.pentecostalpublishing.com

Library of Congress Cataloging-in-Publication Data

DeMerchant, Bennie, 1941-
      Full throttle : the missionary story of Bennie and Theresa DeMerchant
      / Bennie DeMerchant and Dolly McElhaney.
            p. cm.
      ISBN 978-1-56722-728-4
      1. DeMerchant, Bennie, 1941- 2. DeMerchant, Theresa. 3.
      Missionaries--Brazil--Biography. 4. Missionaries--United
      States--Biography. 5. United Pentecostal Church
      International--Missions--Brazil. I. McElhaney, Dolly. II. Title.
      BV2853.B7A135 2008
      266'.9940922--dc22
      [B]
                                                            2008037299

In loving memory of
Bennie Jonas DeMerchant
August 8, 1976 - June 15, 1992

Table of Contents

Foreword

A preacher's kid, I grew up hearing the intriguing adventures of Bennie and Theresa DeMerchant's work in the Amazon. We raised money for airplane parts and new engines. We read letters of the growing revival in Manaus, the capital of the Amazon Basin of Brazil. Perhaps these stories and fund-raising efforts fueled my own (later fulfilled) desires to be a pilot and a preacher.

Years later I met Brother DeMerchant for the first time. I was struck by how humble this man is. In my mind he is a giant among men. In his mind he is much different. This man, who is responsible for tens of thousands of souls being saved, is more comfortable in hammocks in the jungle than in hotels in the city. Sleeping on the floor in an airport with the necessary roll to the right and then to the left to avoid the carpet cleaner is sufficient for Bennie. He is comfortable on the floor because he has spent much of his life there, talking to God … his friend.

As our paths began crossing more frequently, I quickly learned that his genius was cocooned in a close relationship with God. He taught me how to catch a peacock bass on a homemade fly and a cane pole. We flew the floatplanes on my faith and his experience when most of the instruments didn't function. He invited me to preach massive conferences in Manaus and treated me as a son. One evening at his house in Manaus, he handed me a bunch of old manuscripts. The paper was faded and the typewritten words blurred by time. He said, "You may enjoy some of these stories if you can't sleep." He was right on both accounts. I enjoyed the stories and I could not sleep until I had read every riveting word. What I read that night is what you will read in the following pages.

I asked Brother DeMerchant why he had never published any of this material. He wondered in his modest way if anyone would be interested. He then explained that he had stopped writing when his only son had died of cancer at a young age. I insisted that my generation and the generation of my sons need to know what God has done and is doing through this amazing life of faith, unfaltering hard work, and unquenchable perseverance in the Amazon. He agreed to start writing again, and, in the talented hands of Dolly McElhaney, the old manuscript has come to life.

I introduce to you a pioneer of Pentecost, a man who has appeared in *Sports Illustrated*, *Field and Stream*, and numerous aeronautical articles while accumulating nearly fifteen thousand hours in the air as pilot in command over the Amazon. Flying to parts unknown and teaching natives how to fish along the way, he witnesses and wins countless souls to Christ. After more than forty years in the Amazon, Brother and Sister DeMerchant are legends in our time. They remain committed to the calling and excited about the future. This book will inspire you and intrigue you. It will capture your imagination and increase your faith. Strap on your seatbelt and get ready for the ride of your life; we're going *Full Throttle*.

—David Myers, JD

Introduction

Following a dream is rarely easy, achieving it is hard work, and it is never done accidentally. Following a calling to perform a missionary ministry seems an impossible task beyond imagination. However, for Bennie and Theresa DeMerchant, that thought never entered their minds as they accepted the challenge of evangelizing the immense Amazon Basin of Brazil, South America.

As a local church pastor, I first met Bennie and Theresa DeMerchant in early 1965 when they were completing their deputation as newly appointed missionaries. As the DeMerchants shared their burden with our congregation that night, it left Sister Scott and me weeping in the altar, forever changed. That night produced in us a missionary call to Ecuador, South America.

The DeMerchants struggled against witchcraft, demon possession, and undreamed-of evil as they reached for the lost of that vast territory. They made headway with a very effective and anointed ministry, opening churches and doing personal evangelism. However, they awakened one morning to the fact that if they trained ten men, who could in turn train one hundred men, they could indeed reach the impossible area of their calling. Over time, their students became teachers, pastors, evangelists, and missionaries to their oncoming generation.

In 1996 I became the DeMerchants' regional director. As I visited them in Manaus, I stood in the pulpits of their local churches filled with congregations that would be termed the heights of success in North America. I studied the immense capacity of those churches and felt a deep sense of awe as I thought, *This is the ministry of a man who has poured a living legacy into the evangelization of the Amazon Basin.*

Theresa, a concert pianist, and Bennie, who could have enjoyed a lucrative life as a commercial pilot, traded the grand piano and the earned wings for a Bible school lectern and a wooden pulpit to evangelize a people to whom God had called them. From the cement sidewalks of the city of Manaus to the depths of steaming jungle trails accessible only by the SFC floatplane, Bennie and Theresa have served to effectively reach their world with the gospel.

Today the United Pentecostal Church International stands tall in the Amazon Basin and all of Brazil. It didn't happen by saying a prayer one evening and awakening to find excellence on the doorstep the next morning. It happened because they gave of themselves to fill the minds of young men and women with God's Word, thus providing hope for as many tomorrows as God will provide Brazil!

—Daniel Scott

Clipped Wings

"Gerald, the plane is in a dive! We've lost fifteen hundred feet of altitude! We have dropped below three thousand feet!" As Bennie DeMerchant glanced at the climb indicator, what he saw made his heart race and sweat bead his upper lip. He knew that the Appalachian Mountains over which they were flying often thrust more than three thousand feet into the air.

"Fly the plane, Bennie," Gerald Grant ordered. "You have some instrument training. I don't."

Bennie and Gerald, longtime friends from Perth, New Brunswick, Canada, and currently living in Saint Paul, Minnesota, had decided to fly Gerald's plane to their respective Canadian families during the April 19, 1962, Easter break at the Apostolic Bible Institute (ABI). Bennie, with seventy hours of total flying time, eagerly rode in the copilot's seat.

Behind the two, three-year-old Ann Grant slept sweetly, curled up into the back seat.

Bennie's instrument training was only instruction on how to operate an aircraft by instruments in level flight without seeing the ground in deteriorating visibility. *It's just enough to get the pilot turned around and headed out of bad weather!* Bennie thought as he took control of the plane, concentrating on dropping no lower. *But how do I turn around? I have no idea what direction I'm flying in. And I don't care what direction I'm flying in as long as it's not too far east and we don't fly over the Atlantic at night and run out of fuel. What if we slam into the hills below us?*

Bennie palmed the throttle with his left hand and pushed on it. The gallant little plane responded and began to climb. With each passing minute, flying conditions deteriorated exponentially. Dense fog and gathering darkness threatened them. No one spoke. Nothing interrupted the droning of the single engine. To Bennie, however, the engine seemed to be laboring, working hard to cut through the thick fog that curled through the wing struts. *Lord, if You'll get us out of this mess, I'll never fly an airplane again!* Bennie prayed. *I'm too young to die. I'm only twenty-one. Theresa and I have only been married a few months. She's too young to be a widow. I've nearly finished three years of Bible school training. I've seen Your hand on my life and heard Your voice in my heart. Am I not going to be able to fulfill the calling You gave me?*

As the plane gained altitude, Bennie slanted a look at Gerald. *He's probably thinking of Eleanor and Ann,* Bennie thought. *O Lord, please! You'll be a great God if You let us land safely.*

Bennie's thoughts whirled faster than the plane's propeller. When he finally spoke, his voice had a raspy edge to it. "Gerald, grab a chart and let's see if we can figure out where we are!"

Gerald flipped through several visual sectional charts that he had flown across and folded during the long day. Under the dim red glow of the overhead cockpit light, his hands trembled in the turbulence from the clouds the airplane bored through. He tried to trace the route they were taking. No visual ground landmarks helped the two orient themselves to the charts as the plane groped through gray fog as thick as wool, as encompassing as a blanket.

"I don't know where we are," Gerald finally admitted, "except that we're about an hour east of Albany."

The thunder of his racing heartbeat nearly drowning the chugging of the engine, Bennie snatched a look outside. *Lord, please!*

Eternity, measured in nanoseconds, filtered past. Tension knotted in Bennie's stomach and whitened the knuckles of his clenched fists. Gerald resumed piloting the plane and concentrated on navigating the craft by the six precious, life-keeping flight instruments. He put the plane into a series of "S" turns as they peered through the side windows, looking for a break in the clouds that snapped through the wing struts.

"Gerald, there's a break!" Bennie nearly shouted. "Over there!"

"I see it!" Gerald exclaimed. "I'm going down."

Thank You, Lord. Backing off on the power, Gerald banked the plane and slid it into a rift in the fog. He cut power further to idle and circled lower. The sight below discouraged them. A winding, traffic-laden highway curved beneath them, and they needed a straightaway to land.

"What do we do, Gerald?" Bennie asked. "Do we go on, return through the soup to Albany if we can find it in the darkness, or try to land on that strip of road full of cars and loaded trucks?"

"We can't go back," Gerald decided. "The risk in landing on the road we can see is less than the risk of skimming the top of a mountain we can't see. We'll fly along it. Maybe it straightens out somewhere."

Gerald dropped the plane lower and circled the area. Wisps of fog flipped past under the plane. A light, misty rain sprinkled the windshield, flattened into water streaks, and blew around it. Cars traveled the highway, too close to each other to allow space and time for the plane to land. When a straight stretch of pavement finally appeared, Bennie's heart sank further.

A guardrail ran along the right side beneath tall light poles standing like sentinels. On the left, a sheer rock face rose abruptly.

It's not airport width, but at least the road's relatively straight, Bennie thought. He noticed two drive-offs over culverts along the right side beyond the straight stretch. *Maybe after we land we can pull into one of those drive-offs and overnight there. With the cooperation of local officials, we might be able to take off at dawn.*

Gerald circled the plane again.

And again. Slowly. Giving traffic time to clear. *Please, Lord, landing space.*

"Hold on," Gerald said through his teeth. "We're going down. Now!"

The Cessna's landing lights beamed a swath above the telephone poles as he centered the plane over the yellow dividing line of the highway. The plane barely skimmed the wires strung on the poles, and then the plane's tires hissed on the highway, fighting for purchase, as Gerald applied the brakes.

The headlights of an approaching car suddenly blazed at the other end of the straightaway.

"Gerald! A car!" Bennie yelled.

"I see it!" Gerald acknowledged and guided the plane to the right, sacrificing the centerline.

The plane struck the road, bounced, and slewed sideways as the right wing clipped the guardrail. A shriek of tearing metal and the acrid smell of tires losing their tread filled the cabin. Bennie's head struck the instrument panel, and stars danced before his eyes as the aircraft careened along the asphalt, its nose on the right shoulder of the road, its right wing against the pavement, and its left wing pointing upward.

Flames crackled from the front engine compartment, and smoke drifted into the cabin.

Ann's screams shrilled into Bennie's ears.

"Gerald, my door's jammed against the pavement!"

Hurry! Hurry!

Gerald snapped off the master switch and struggled to open his door against the weight of gravity. After what seemed a lifetime, he was able to scramble out.

Hurry! Hurry! The smoke is getting denser.

Bennie turned and unbuckled a sobbing Ann, holding her tightly as he inched the two of them up through the narrow, confining space and out the door.

Aviation fuel leaked, flowing from a ruptured gas line. The steel cable guardrail that ran through drilled steel posts had chewed through the cowling of the white-and-red Cessna 172 and pounded the carburetor and exhaust system beneath it. The beautiful aluminum bird with N-8947B painted on its fuselage lay crippled on the road.

"Are you all right?" Gerald gasped.

"Yeah. Just shaken up. Bent my glasses. You okay?"

The fuselage and the tail, canted at a forty-five-degree angle from the shoulder of the road to its centerline, effectively blocked the highway. The right and front landing gear had buckled. Cable from the guardrail had snarled around the propeller. Skid marks had temporarily squeegeed the pavement. But they were alive. Badly shaken and teeth chattering, they were nonetheless alive and mobile.

So was a quick-thinking semi truck driver caught in the traffic piling up in both directions. He snatched a fire extinguisher from the cab of his truck, braved the fire in the front of the plane, and doused the flames. Another trucker cradled little Ann, speaking softly to her. Sirens wailed the arrival of police cars and an ambulance. Red, rotating lights turned the faces of curious onlookers off and on.

"Mister, get away!" a policeman shouted as an onlooker ran toward the wreckage. "Don't you see the spilled gas?"

The onlooker scurried away from the spilled gas, his lit cigarette dangling from his lip.

"Is anyone hurt?" the police officer asked kindly. After seeing that no one was injured, he led the trio to his cruiser. "I need to see your documents."

With the fire now out, Bennie crawled back into the plane and retrieved the aircraft registration, airworthiness certificate, log books, radio license, and pilot and medical certificates. The policeman asked the two men dozens of questions as Gerald comforted Ann.

Finally, when the police finished their interrogation, the two men had a question of their own. "Where are we?"

They were on Route 13 near Fitchburg, Massachusetts, only a short distance south of their flight plan. During the long police interrogation, crews arrived to dismantle the wreckage. The wrecking crew removed the crumpled wing and fuselage from the highway and deposited the pathetic parts behind the Lunenburg Airport hangar. Then the police took Bennie, Gerald, and Ann to a local hotel.

Bennie never forgot that night. Still badly shaken, he spent the dark hours pouring praise and thanksgiving from his heart to God. Scenes flashed before his eyes: the thick, ropy, endless fog flipping by the plane; the narrow opening in the clouds; the traffic-laden highway; the asphalt rising to meet the aircraft; the glistening wires of the telephone posts on the right coming up to meet them; small flames darting from the front compartment; the awful devastation to the plane; the cable from the uprooted guardrail entwined in the propeller; the red lights pulsing over the crowd of curious onlookers.

These sights rolled through his brain again and again, and then …

… then Bennie saw, instead of scenes from the plane wreck, a relief map of the Amazon River system in northern Brazil. It also lay in the dark shadows of night. Scattered along the globe's largest water drainage system, little lighthouses appeared from the shadows of the map, their tiny beams twinkling in the blackness.

A voice spoke to him. "I have saved your life for a purpose!"

There, in a strange hotel room, God forcefully reaffirmed Bennie's call to be a missionary to this huge area of Brazil's rain forest. In the tough times ahead when it seemed that all else failed, Bennie would remember that dream and that voice. God had His own navigational chart for Bennie's life.

And He had started Bennie on that course when Bennie was but a child.

Tug o' War

Bennie's first recollection of God tugging on his life was at Upper Kent, a small town fifteen miles below his home in Perth, New Brunswick, Canada. A young minister, Percy Robertson, was holding tent meetings in the summer of 1948, and Bennie's parents drove their family to one of the evening services. Seven-year-old Bennie listened attentively to the message on the crucifixion of Jesus. At the close of the meeting, the little boy walked down the sawdust-covered aisle and knelt on the boards in front of the altar. He wept and prayed, and when he got up he felt clean inside.

Bennie's pastor, Brother William Rolston, was a missions-minded man who loved helping missionaries fulfill their call to foreign lands. One night a few months after Bennie's trek to the altar, a foreign missionary spoke in a church service. He enthralled the young Bennie as he told stories of his experiences on the mission field.

When his mom and dad got into the car, Bennie learned from their conversation that the visiting missionaries would be coming with the pastor to the family home before returning to Plaster Rock.

After I go to bed, the missionaries will be in the living room having coffee and sandwiches, Bennie thought, *but I want to hear some more missionary stories.*

Immediately after arriving home, Bennie slipped into the living room, climbed over the sofa in a corner by the fireplace, and curled up on the floor. From there he could learn more about this most interesting preacher from foreign lands. The next morning Bennie's mother looked all over the house to find Bennie to get him ready for school. By the time she found him asleep behind the sofa, she scolded him because he would be late.

Foreign missions interest started out as a curiosity but later became one of the boy's main interests. If a person asked the eight-year-old what he wanted to be when he grew up, he would answer, "A missionary." He loved watching the slides of foreign fields and believers as the images were projected onto a screen or wall. And Thursday, Foreign Missions Day during the annual convention at Plaster Rock, was, to him, one of the year's most exciting days.

Three memorable and prophetic things happened to Bennie during his tenth year. First, he got a paper route delivering the *Telegraph Journal,* a daily paper printed in Saint John, New Brunswick. It introduced him to the responsibility of operating his own business and kept him busy building up the customer base and delivering over one hundred papers on his bike in Perth.

The second event was Bennie's baptism. Pastor Rolston stood in a lightweight white suit in the middle of the Tobique River near the CNR train bridge in Plaster Rock, New Brunswick, on the second Sunday of July 1951.

"Brother Bennie, do you intend to live for God the rest of your life?" he asked.

Bennie nodded his head and felt his pastor's hand tighten on the back of his neck. Pastor Rolston clutched Bennie's hands crossed on his chest and baptized the young boy in the name of Jesus Christ for the remission of his sins!

The third outstanding event was a dream in which Bennie was standing on a floating raft of logs in a huge, wide river. He gazed around. Lowlands spread on the right, and distant, rolling, jungle-covered hills rose on his left. He looked down and noticed a distinct difference in the color of the water on both sides of the raft. One side was black, the other brown. As far as he could see, the waters flowed ahead of him side by side without mixing. That was all! What a strange dream!

As he grew older, Bennie acquired an array of skills that later would prove useful and even life saving. To keep his four sons out of mischief on long summer days, Harold DeMerchant introduced them to fly-fishing Atlantic salmon. One day Mr. DeMerchant took Bennie to a well-known barber, who taught the teen how to tie salmon flies. Bennie soon could tie any salmon fly pattern on the river. In fly-tying, he strayed from usual patterns and experimented by mixing up colors and materials on a fly he knew already worked. He then tested the "new" fly among others fishing the river. When he produced a new pattern that hooked fish, he had a chance to make a few bucks!

Later, Mr. DeMerchant bought potato farms near Beechwood, New Brunswick. There, Bennie learned to work with farm tractors and their implements and to avoid their risks of operation. Working in his mother's food store, he also learned more about running a business: dealing with wholesalers, the staff, advertising, competition, customers, stretching a dollar to pay bills, and making a profit. This early training prepared Bennie for the business aspect and endless red tape he would encounter on the mission field.

A flying service with three or four small airplanes opened up nearby on McCrea flat. The senior DeMerchant invested in the firm, hoping to rent planes at good rates. One day Bennie got his first plane ride. The two-place plane ran like a sewing machine. When Bennie returned from the short flight, he was determined that one day he was going to fly airplanes. Thoughts of being a missionary fled his mind. He would be a pilot!

From then on, a goodly portion of Bennie's earnings from mowing lawns, picking potatoes, or working at the store went for plane rides. He would pedal his bike from Perth to the P&M flying service in Fort Fairfield, Maine, to pay an instructor to take him up flying for half an hour or an hour and, at times, let him feel the controls of an airplane.

Ralph and Gerald Grant, bosom buddies of the DeMerchant tribe, stayed at the DeMerchants' house often and tinkered with old cars. Before long, Bennie had mastered the basic principles of gas-powered engines.

Bennie learned to swim when young and could swim all afternoon without touching bottom, flipping over and resting on his back in the water.

Once, while the church held a Sunday school picnic at a campsite below Perth, a high-speed motorboat overturned with a small boy on board. Others nearby, hearing the screams, called Bennie to help. He spotted the problem in the river and stripped off his clothes while running down the bank. A young boy clung to a small point of the bow of the submerged boat, and Bennie swam out to help. Slowly, he and the boat operator got the youngster safely back to shore to the mounted police and a waiting crowd. Bennie waited in the water until someone found his scattered clothes.

When Bennie entered high school, he discovered his favorite subjects: shop, geometry, and trigonometry. *If I know this well, I can become an engineer and draw building plans and earn good money,* he mused as he bent over the drawing board. *I love this algebra and trig stuff, too. Airplane pilots have to be able to use math,* he thought as he pondered equations. Career workshops at school presented the good side of many future fields. Bennie attended some of these seminars at school and even questioned his previous missionary inclinations. At times he asked himself, "Was all that wanting to be a missionary based on feelings, dreams, emotions, and kid stuff?"

Then, on the fifth of July, 1957, at the usual convention in Plaster Rock, Bennie received the baptism of the Holy Ghost, speaking in other tongues for the first time in his life! The late Verner Larsen, missionary to Colombia, remained praying with him till three o'clock in the morning. This powerful experience was very real, and Bennie could hardly believe that he had received something so simple yet so satisfying.

A few months after Bennie received the baptism of the Holy Ghost, Sister Nilah Rutledge came to the church on the hill in Perth to hold a series of special meetings. She preached a convicting consecration message in a Sunday morning service and made an appeal for people to give their lives to God.

"Is there someone here who will come forward?" she asked the congregation, which had risen to its feet.

No one moved.

Sister Nilah stood in a loose white dress, her face anxious and pleading. "Is there someone here who would come forward and place your life on the altar for God's will and work to be done in you?"

Tears streamed down Bennie's face as his ambitions played tug o' war against the call from the altar.

With an outstretched arm, she queried softly, "Is there one?"

Loud and clear on the inside, Bennie heard, "I need you!"

God had spoken. The whims of ever becoming an engineer or airline pilot blew away like dandelion fluff on a stiff breeze.

That was it. Bennie knew it. He stood alone weeping at the front of the church altar, totally surrendered to irreversibly follow Jesus to wherever He led. The teenager spent the rest of the day crying and praying in his bedroom, but he knew from that time on that he would not worry about a career! He was confident that God would work His will out in his life step by step as he walked along. But he also wondered what that next step would be.

Bennie's pastors, William J. and Sadie Rolston

Home of Harold and Beatrice DeMerchant
(1945-59) Perth, New Brunswick, Canada

Harold Jr., Jackalene, Bennie (1944)

Flight
Preparations

Bennie loved his dad dearly. Harold DeMerchant was Bennie's idol and image of what a father ought to be. He worked hard and played hard after the work was done. He always made church services a priority and planned his activities around them, trundling his six children to church whether they wanted to go or not! He insisted that his youngsters finish their homework early on church nights. He loved his wife and all of his children and had a heavy hand in discipline at times, especially if he discovered willful disobedience.

"He could be tolerant if he knew you did the wrong thing through ignorance, and when he disciplined us, he would always let us know why," Bennie recalls.

One example of Bennie's relationship with his dad is illustrated by a simple incident one hot summer day when Bennie was pedaling his bike to the Goodine homestead from Perth to Tilley among the high hills. His dad appeared with the Chrysler and stopped.

"You going to Grandma's?" he inquired.

"Yeah, Dad!"

DeMerchant looked at the hills ahead. "Bring your bike over closer to the car, Son," he requested.

Bennie complied, and coasted alongside the moving car, sitting on the seat of the bike while his dad's muscular arm held the handlebars. The senior DeMerchant slowly steered the car up and over the steep hills, and when they reached the top, he released Bennie with a "Good-bye, Boy!" and sped off in a cloud of dust!

Bennie's pastor and youth leaders, knowing Bennie's desire to become a missionary, greatly encouraged him. However, most of Bennie's early attempts at preaching crash-landed. In his room under the eaves, he would pray and study, only to lose 80 percent of his thoughts when he stepped behind the pulpit. Then it seemed that Satan whispered in his ear, "You better plan on doing something different with your life, because you'll never be a preacher."

Bennie persevered. He reveled in the times when the Spirit of God touched him and he felt the surge of the power of the anointing. Then the Lord poured Scriptures, thoughts, and incidences into his mind.

Bennie had been asked to preach a youth rally in Mars Hill, Maine, on May 11, 1959. After the service on the way home, as he braked his dad's 1956 Buick at Canadian customs for a routine inspection, the customs officer beckoned to Bennie's passenger and friend, Buddy Goodine, to get out of the car. Off to the side, the officer spoke softly to Buddy.

When Buddy returned to the car, he said, "Bennie, slide over. I'll drive the rest of the way home."

Bennie sensed that something was wrong as Buddy sped along without saying a word. Then, when he saw cars filling the driveway and lining both sides of the street in front of his house on Terrace Street, a dreadful foreboding filled his heart. The big house swarmed with neighbors, close family friends, and relatives.

As Bennie climbed the back steps that led to the kitchen door, his uncle, Herman Taylor, stepped up and put his arm on Bennie's shoulder. In a low voice, he sobbed, "It's your dad. He's gone!"

"Gone? Gone! Gone! Why? Why? Why, Lord?" Bennie sobbed upstairs on his bed. How he would ache in days ahead and repeat those same questions over and over about one person who had such a strong influence on his life and character and whose image he idolized! At eighteen and having three younger siblings in his family, Bennie could present to the Lord many reasons why his dad was still needed!

Bennie's mother was now a forty-five-year-old widow with two businesses to run and a heavy debt from previous losses in the risky potato business. Now she consulted him about businesses Bennie had not even been aware of. Bennie worked as usual in the summer months at the store, stocking shelves, running cash registers, and taking care of fruit and vegetable stands and the meat department. The teenager dealt with wholesalers and customers for a nearly endless month when his mother went into the hospital for surgery. He had to handle the business, bank deposits, and checking accounts. He also managed the staff of eight to twelve people, depending on week or weekend periods. But the experience was invaluable training for a wannabe missionary.

Bennie's bittersweet graduation occurred approximately six weeks after his dad's death. Harold DeMerchant had strongly encouraged Bennie to stay in high school until he graduated and even to enroll in night courses in electricity, typing, and woodworking. After graduating from Southern Victoria Regional High School in Andover, New Brunswick, the summer of 1959, Bennie began to take flying more seriously.

He made his first solo flight nearby in Fort Fairfield, Maine, about two months after his dad's passing. The Aeronca Champ, a sixty-five-horsepower two-seater airplane, bounced all over the narrow landing strip. Bennie's first landing looked like a speeding kangaroo jerking to a stop, and it inspired the instructor to take over the controls! As the little bird idled by the edge of the strip, a dejected Bennie slumped and wondered what went wrong.

"Bennie, don't hurry to land this plane when its wheels come in just above the grass with all that speed," explained the instructor in his calm, deliberate voice. "It will want to fly again. Hold it level, a yard above the ground. Let it slow down. As it sinks to the ground, ease the stick back, way back hard, and hold it there till it settles by itself on all three wheels. Now taxi back to the end and go full throttle again for another touch-and-go!"

After another two hours of takeoffs and landings, enough things went right. The next day, Bennie soloed!

Five weeks later, Bennie left home to enroll at the Apostolic Bible Institute in Saint Paul, Minnesota, where he would begin systematic study toward becoming a minister. While at ABI, Bennie worked as dishwasher, janitor, coal furnace stoker, and just about anything else that Brother S. G. Norris, the head of the school, needed done.

Bennie also helped his lifelong buddy, Gerald Grant, maintain Grant's plane and took advantage of his access to the aircraft to finish his flight training. After Bennie received his private pilot's license October 1, 1961, he was allowed to make long trips, even international flights, and to carry passengers.

Meanwhile, Bennie fell in love.

Theresa Shomberg, an office secretary, was quite businesslike as she accepted Bennie's registration fee, but oh, with such a charming smile! Over the next few weeks, Bennie learned that beyond her secretarial duties for the school's president, Theresa taught English and piano and worked with the music director and choirs.

As Bennie plied his trombone in the school orchestra, he caught himself staring at her fingers as they ran over the ivory keys. By asking around, he discovered that Theresa practiced classical piano music by the day. In 1958, she had come in second place in the state of Minnesota as a pre-virtuoso contestant in a piano concert held at Northrop Auditorium in Minneapolis.

Bennie also learned that when Theresa was seventeen she felt God speak to her heart: "Would you be willing to go to a foreign field?"

She prayed. "Where, Lord?"

Then one word came to her: "Brazil."

She could not get away from it. Every time she prayed, she had to pray for Brazil first. After graduation, she still didn't feel any closer to Brazil, so at Brother Norris's request, she stayed in Saint Paul and worked in the school. She knew that if God wanted her in Brazil, He would open the door in His own good time.

Shortly after Bennie arrived at ABI, he testified that he enrolled in ABI because he wanted to be a missionary to Brazil.

"Theresa took note of that," Bennie observes. "I was only eighteen, but she said I was a hard worker, a go-getter, and someone who knew where he was going. She liked someone who, she said, could make decisions and stick to them. She loved the challenge of exciting ventures and someone who was thrilled by the great outdoors.

"We knew we were one of a kind, and God put us together," Bennie summarizes.

The friendship grew and romance developed. Brother Norris married them on July 22, 1961, in Saint Paul, Minnesota. Now, forty-seven years later, they both continue to thank God for intertwining the threads of their lives. But snags developed when the young couple tried to weave Brazil into the tapestry.

The
Proving Ground

Brazil waved before Bennie and Theresa like a beckoning banner. The enormous country, the size of the entire United States plus a second Texas, had only three missionary families. The Sam Bakers, the John Lambeths, and the Robert Norrises had established small but solid works in the southern part of the country. But the state of Amazonas, five percent larger than Alaska, covered by the world's largest standing forest, drained by the earth's mightiest river, and occupying roughly half of Brazil, captured the yearning of their hearts.

Bennie and Theresa, however, both knew that proofs of their ministry were prerequisites to their going to Brazil. The Sunday following Bennie's graduation from ABI in Saint Paul, Minnesota, in May 1962, Brother A. W. Post installed Bennie as pastor of the church of about three families in River de Chute, New Brunswick, Canada.

The De Merchants gaped in dismay at their living quarters in River de Chute. Theresa remembers the place very well:

> Someone had moved an old house next to the church to be used for the parsonage. The floor had worms running in it. It had no basement, so we had to build one of cement. It had no furnace, so we bought a used one but had to put in wood to burn at 3 AM or there was no heat.
>
> In winter when I got up to wash, the washcloth was frozen to the sink. We had no appliances, so we bought a little camp stove, and a refrigerator to keep things from freezing as all of January it was around -30 degrees. The snow was piled to our roof. We had a path to our outhouse, which offered a ring of ice to sit on. We carried water from our neighbors up a big hill until we got water piped in.
>
> We both worked in my mother-in-law's food store all week, got up early on Sunday mornings to gather children for Sunday school, sometimes in a sleigh with horses. I gave piano lessons in my spare time. After a year, we thankfully moved to a more liveable place.

By purchasing an old bus and canvassing the entire area, they were able to fill the bus and bring young people to Sunday school and even to church services. People from the area began to drop into the meetings, and attendance rose from in the twenties and thirties to the eighties and, at peak times, to 120.

In August of 1963, Brother W. J. Rolston invited the duo to move to Plaster Rock to assist him in pastoring three churches in the area while he and Sister Rolston spent the winter in Ireland with relatives. Bennie and Theresa lived in the church parsonage and ministered in the New Denmark, Tilley, and Plaster Rock Pentecostal Churches. Theresa also worked with music and the youth in the church and taught music at Plaster Rock public school.

As busy and fulfilling as their lives were, they still yearned to be on the field of their calling. They made the long trip from Plaster Rock to Memphis, Tennessee, in 1963 to meet with the Foreign Missions Board at the General Conference. They were turned down. Disappointed, they returned to Canada with one consolation: they had registered their intentions to go to Brazil.

In the summer of 1964, Brother Rolston invited Brother Oscar Vouga, Director of Foreign Missions, to preach the Plaster Rock annual church convention. Brother Vouga asked to meet Bennie and Theresa in the Rolstons' living room. The subject? Brazil. Brother Vouga's greatest concern was whether they were just going to "try out being missionaries" or whether they would make Brazil their serious lifetime work.

"Theresa, I feel we should meet the Foreign Missions Board again," Bennie told Theresa later. Both of them had spent many hours in prayer over Brazil.

Theresa needed no convincing, even though the trip to San Antonio, Texas, the next year would be especially grueling for her because she was expecting their first child. Driving from New Brunswick to San Antonio in their Volkswagen "Bug," they sometimes bought gas at nineteen cents a gallon. Political posters along the way urged voters to choose Barry Goldwater or Lyndon Johnson for the next United States President.

To stretch their meager supply of dollars, they alternated sleeping in a motel and the VW, using an ingenious system Bennie devised. He would pull the car into a cotton field after dark, slide the bucket seats off their rails, remove the small back seat, and insert a plywood floor on the bottom of the vehicle. Inflatable air mattress and sleeping bags comprised their beds. By dawn they would be on their way again, having an early breakfast at a restaurant where they could wash their faces.

After four days of traveling, the pair reached San Antonio. There Bennie was ordained to ministry by General Superintendent A. T. Morgan. They felt blessed to have the chance to present themselves to the Foreign Missions Board again. With their questioning finished, Bennie and Theresa left the room. They wouldn't know the verdict until the upcoming Missionary Sunday at the conference. How could they live that long in such unbearable tension and suspense?

On Saturday night, before the Sunday Foreign Missions service at General Conference, Brother Paul Box approached Bennie and Theresa. Bennie's heart began to pound. *Lord, is this the time? No person so young has ever been appointed as a career missionary to the field! Will this be it? What will he say? Will we have to wait another year and come back as we laboriously did this year, or is it now?*

Then with a big smile, Brother Box said, "You folks have been appointed as missionaries to Brazil! Come back tomorrow night to this back stage to enter to sit on the platform as we direct."

Bennie and Theresa, almost speechless with joy and delight, hugged him. Then they turned and hugged every other missionary they could find. This was it! That two-minute meeting behind the stage was their School of Missions training, their missions manual, and their deputation handbook. The Partners In Missions program had not yet been dreamed of. No national or district mission coordinators existed to help smooth their way.

After returning to Plaster Rock, Theresa continued to teach in the local school until the end of the year. The serious business of raising airfare, shipping costs, and daily living expenses was the most important part of a missionary's work before he could go to the field of his calling. Before Partners In Missions and planned budgets, a missionary was required to raise his fare to travel and live on the field supported by designated funds. When the Foreign Mission Department did not get enough designated funds, they used undesignated funds that could also be sent to the missionary.

They zigzagged around the country in their Volkswagen Bug, visiting churches' missions conferences and pouring out their burden for Brazil.

Then, unknown to them, a "Don't invite Bennie to preach" blitz began in Canada.

Bewildered that he was not being invited to minister in most of his home district, Bennie drove deep into the United States to garner support. He did not know that an ex-Foreign Missions Director who opposed Bennie's appointment to Brazil sent letters to ministers in his home district. Bennie opened his copy of a circular letter that indicated he was sent a copy, but it had been deliberately mailed several weeks later than the others. The door had been shut on his deputation in the New Brunswick he loved!

The letter reached him just minutes before service in Saint Louis, Missouri. Staggered by the information, he wept at the tricks and treachery that had been used against a young minister from their midst in New Brunswick, but he forced a cheerful expression on his face and kept the contents of the devastating letter to himself.

As he stood in the pulpit of Brother Harry Branding's church in Saint Louis, preparing to minister, a message in tongues burst forth from the congregation. Brother Branding walked to Bennie and from behind placed his hands on the new missionary's shoulders and prophesied.

"I have many souls in the land where I called you. You will face many problems! Be strong, and be of good courage for I have many waiting for the message! Fear not! Be strong! Be of good courage! The brethren there and all the brethren here will know that I called you and I sent you to this land!"

Bennie, remembering the letter he'd opened just before the beginning of the service, bowed his head and cried at the pulpit after hearing such a powerful confirmation from an elderly man of God!

Bennie and Theresa had now been married for four years, and the Lord gave them a baby girl on April 27, 1965. Bennie was alone on much of the deputation trail and raced home after service in nearby Maine to see his new daughter, Beth, in the Plaster Rock hospital.

A flurry of activity followed. They applied and received their passports: Bennie's from Ottawa, Canada, Theresa's from Bangor, Maine. They sold all their bulky, expensive-to-ship furniture; they would replace these articles once they reached Manaus. They crated and shipped their bed and eight barrels of clothes, ministerial books, plenty of canned baby food, small household appliances, dishes, footwear, and a host of miscellaneous items. A ship embarking from New York would take their goods to New Orleans and transfer them to a Booth Lines ship going on to Manaus, a thousand miles up the Amazon River. They started their permanent visa process and were given permanent residence stamps for Brazil in the late summer of 1965.

Their farewell service time had come: October 25, 1965. Pastor Rolston didn't hide his forebodings about what the young couple would do when they arrived in Manaus, Brazil.

"Bennie, you and Theresa are going to a place completely unknown to you," he said, his face mirroring his concern. "You don't know anyone there. You don't speak a word of Portuguese. How are you going to manage finding a place to live? Buying food? Getting from place to place?"

Then Pastor Rolston requested that the congregation stand and pray that these problems would all work out and that the young missionaries would make good contacts from the beginning.

Bennie's sobbing widow-mother stood by the boarding gate the next morning in the airport in Bangor, Maine, while they prepared to board the Northeast Airline flight to Boston, then Miami, and on to Brazil.

But the promise of the Lord still stands, Bennie thought, quoting to himself from Mark 10:29-30 as he comforted his weeping mother. *There is no man that hath left house, or brethren, or sisters, or father, or mother, or wife, or children, or lands, for my sake, and the gospel's, but he shall receive an hundredfold now in this time, ... and in the world to come eternal life.*

Bennie, Theresa, and baby Beth reached Belem at the mouth of the Amazon River in northern Brazil, one thousand miles east of Manaus, at three o'clock in the morning. They had left northern Maine on a cold, snowy day and landed in a jungle city a few miles from the equator at sea level. When they stepped from the plane into the rather primitive airport, hot, heavy, moist air enveloped them. Even breathing was difficult.

"It's like a sauna!" Theresa gasped. "What is it going to be like in the day, when the sun comes up?"

After they checked through customs and immigration, the airline took them to the airline's guest house, a little white cement structure with narrow, hard beds and a miniature air conditioner that rattled loudly. There they spent a restless night, nearly overwhelmed by fatigue, heat, and humidity.

At that time, Manaus was not connected to the outside world with international flights, and flights from Belem to Manaus were often happenstance. Two days later they boarded a four-engine domestic propeller plane for Manaus, finally arriving at their base city on October 29, 1965. The prayers offered in Canada about getting the right contacts seemed to be answered. In less than forty-eight hours after having arrived in Manaus as a total stranger, Bennie had established a casual friendship with two young men about his own age—each of whom later became elected as mayor of this city of 200,000 people.

About two weeks later, a young tour guide who spoke English asked Bennie to visit the main tourist attraction of Manaus by boat.

"It is to see the meeting of the waters," he explained. "Very important. Very impressive. You must see it."

Bennie accepted. Just eight miles below Manaus, the mighty Negro River flows into the mightier Amazon. Together they continue their final one-thousand-mile journey to the South Atlantic Ocean, pushing fresh water two hundred miles into the sea.

Bennie perched on a side seat and watched the other passengers as the boat ploughed the black water of the Negro River. As it approached the chocolate brown water of the Amazon coming in from the south, Bennie got up and went to stand on the bow of the boat and looked downriver in amazement.

What he had seen as a ten-year-old child in a dream fourteen years earlier coincided with what he saw as he looked downriver. To his left rose the distant higher rise of land. Two very different, very distinct colors pouring from the great rivers coursed side by side downstream for as far as he could see.

As he stared at the unmingling water, a strange, warm feeling suffused him. *Lord, I am standing here in Your most perfect will!* he thought.

Though he was new in this city with few friends, his close relatives and relatives in the Lord afar off, Bennie's faith soared. This confirmation of a fourteen-year-old dream energized him and acted like a gyroscopic compass that remains pointing on the same plane when the storms and turbulence in life roll.

Bennie clung to that confirmation during the weeks and months ahead when frustrations followed, often in waves, sometimes in billows.

Goodbye, folks! Manaus-bound!

Meeting of the Negro and Amazon Rivers near
Manaus, Brazil

Aliens in a Strange Land

"There's not much to choose from, is there?" Bennie observed to Brother Sam Baker, his missionary supervisor from São Paulo, as Bennie and Theresa shopped for furniture for the small apartment they had rented after staying in Hotel Amazonas for a week.

The DeMerchants bought a new refrigerator. To their dismay, it did not work. Unable to speak Portuguese, they trundled back and forth by rented pickup truck to the store, trying to explain the dilemma. Baby Beth needed milk. Finally the store sent a used, dirty refrigerator from storage to their narrow apartment, and took their "new" one for repairs. They understood that after a month, the store would bring their "new" repaired refrigerator back.

When Bennie opened the refrigerator door, big cockroaches scurried out in every direction.

Theresa screamed as Bennie tried to catch the wily insects. They had never seen a cockroach in Wisconsin or Canada.

When the new-but-repaired refrigerator was finally returned to them, it continually needed repairs. The store manager had taken advantage of them as foreigners unable to speak Portuguese without an interpreter. He had sold them a "new" refrigerator that they picked out at the show-case in the store, but he delivered one from his service shop that had been used, repossessed, and repainted.

The small, $75-per-month apartment on 215 Getulio Vargas Street shared walls with buildings on each side. Without side windows, the apartment had no ventilation unless the front and back doors were opened and the wind blew from the right direction. A high wall enclosing a cemetery topped a steep bank on the opposite side of street. The crest of the wall formed their horizon. On early-morning prayer walks, Bennie could walk around the cemetery and see painted concrete statues of saints interspersed among the tombs of the poor and the miniature cathedrals of the rich.

One night after they retired, Theresa kept gagging. She felt her throat was full. She kept swallowing and swallowing, but whatever it was, it would not go down. Finally, she reached into her throat with her fingers, pulled out a five-inch white worm, and threw it on Bennie's pillow.

She screamed in horror, "Turn on the light!"

A sleepy-eyed Bennie replied, "Oh, that's just a white shoelace."

"It's not, Ben. It's wiggling!"

Slumber took wings.

"Bennie, how many more of those gruesome parasites are in my stomach?" she worried.

They captured the worm, placed it in a bottle, and took it to the doctor the next day. He prescribed medicine for ascaris for Theresa and year-old Beth. It was an unpleasant way to learn to make a monthly trip to the laboratory for a checkup.

Four months after their arrival in Manaus, they received more-than-welcome news: Sheaves For Christ had raised funds to purchase a Jeep station wagon for them. Until then, they'd had four choices for transportation: rental car, taxi, bus, or feet.

"There's a downside to this," Bennie told Theresa. "I have to fly to São Paulo to get it. The difference between buying it here and in São Paulo close to the factory is about two thousand dollars. I'll have to leave you here alone with the baby."

Theresa, with her always-able-to-cope personality, saw instantly the advantage of Bennie's flying to São Paulo. "You can go to the conference and buy the Jeep at the same time," she replied.

At the end of the conference, Sam Baker and Bennie drove the Jeep Rural to Belem at the mouth of the Amazon, where it was put on a barge. Fourteen days later it arrived one thousand miles upriver in Manaus. No more taxis, rental cars, or buses for them! And they realized a savings in shoe leather, too!

For eight months they sweltered in their tiny, suffocatingly hot apartment and concentrated on breaking the back of Portuguese, studying mornings, afternoons, and evenings with several private teachers, going over verb conjugations and vocabulary building nonstop. And they waged a fruitless war against thievery.

One Sunday night, weary from nearly constant study of Portuguese, they visited an evangelical church. They wanted to get out and hear Christian songs. Maybe the melodies would be familiar, and they might be able to understand some of the words.

But regardless of beliefs, the DeMerchants just did not fit into their formal, militaristic mode of worship that prohibited anyone from clapping his hands even on faster songs. At the end of the service, the pastor said to Bennie, "You are not welcome here. Do not come back; do not visit any of the members of this church. There are over a hundred different kinds of Protestant missions and churches in Manaus. Why don't you take your message to the jungle?"

On returning to the apartment, they found a broken window. Their next-door neighbor, the son of a policeman, had stolen several personal items. The police did nothing. Often the police knew who broke into houses but just shrugged their shoulders. Justice existed symbolically.

Before the DeMerchants' first year ended, thieves broke into their home five times. Theresa's accordion, a Wollensak tape recorder, even Bennie's old pickup truck fell prey to thieves. To top it off, the truck was stolen in front of the house an hour before the local police went on a strike for a long weekend! Weeks later, driving alone on a road through the jungle out of town, Bennie spotted it from the Jeep. Bennie reported the matter to the police. Though he saw it on the road two or three more times and the police promised on the phone to check into it, they did nothing.

Tired of making phone calls, Bennie visited their office. The police could not find the report Bennie had made the night it was stolen since the page of the cheap school scribbler where such reports were recorded had obviously been torn out.

About three o'clock one morning nearly a year after their arrival, Ben was awakened by a foreign sound in the room. At first, he thought he was seeing a long, slender shadow from the window over his head. Nothing in the room made a similar shadow when car lights passed on the street. That "shadow" turned out to be a stiff, slender stick with a nail curved upward on its tapered end. It was tailored especially for its purpose. Before Bennie fully awakened, it had caught Theresa's purse and fished it out through the horizontal slots of the steel-framed window slats opened for ventilation. Manipulated by a brawny-armed man, the stick returned to snag Bennie's trousers containing his pocketed wallet near the bed. Bennie quickly sensed what was going on. He lay still, pondering his next move.

Then he yelled in Portuguese, "Woman, pass me that thirty-eight revolver! Quick!"

The long stick and his trousers dropped beside the bed, and the thief took off, running toward an alley behind the house.

Months after police investigated an earlier break-in of their house, two polite, plainclothes policemen presented their identification.

"Sir, we were sent to verify the registration numbers of a firearm you have in your possession," they told him.

Bennie produced his documents and dug his new 30-06 Winchester hunting rifle out of a closet. Bennie planned to take it on jungle trips for protection when in the wild. Bennie had included this rifle in his consular list of baggage and registered it with the local police on arrival.

"All is in order," they declared, "but we are surprised that all numbers bear out. We must show this to our superior in the office downtown. However, you may carry the gun and go with us, and when our superior officer checks that all is in order, you may return with your rifle."

Bennie complied, but when the trio arrived at the office, the needed officer was "out" and would return "shortly." Bennie waited till noon, but the officer did not appear.

The officers put the rifle in their locker. "Come back later this afternoon," the men told him.

Bennie was given no receipt for the firearm. After repeated visits and one even with the American consular representative, he was told that they had made a mistake in allowing him to have the rifle and he would not see it again.

He didn't. Until then Bennie had loved firearms, but he had to consider himself in a foreign country and comply as a good guest. Although these intermittent robberies frustrated him and the lack of justice hammered at him, Bennie felt he represented a higher work than fighting some smaller things no matter how unjust they seemed. Bigger things lay ahead. With the help of the Lord, he stifled his anger, trusting that God would pay him back down the road.

After eight months of renting a small apartment, the DeMerchants moved into an abandoned construction that they purchased and finished on Ramos Ferreira Street near downtown Manaus. They reinforced their doors and windows with iron gratings and bought a German shepherd dog which they named Pastor. That seemed to solve the thievery problem.

As he worked with bricklayers and their assistants, overseeing things and helping here and there on his own house, Bennie gathered a lot of information about using local materials for construction. He soon became fluent in Portuguese. While he learned construction and mechanical vocabulary, Theresa quickly expanded her vocabulary into childcare and homemaking areas.

By an uncomfortable experience, Bennie learned to pay attention to applying the accent on the correct syllable. One day, after feeling quite fluent from several months of study with tutors and shopping on their own at the markets, Bennie entered an ice cream shop. High school students who dropped by for a sundae or an ice cream cone chattered away, filling most of the metal folding tables and chairs.

A neatly dressed woman in a white cap and uniform appeared from behind the counter with an ice cream scoop in her hand. She pointed to the list of flavors above her head and waited for his selection.

Bennie wanted coconut ice cream, but said the word with the accent on the second syllable instead of the first.

With a strange smile, the young woman questioned, "What?"

He repeated his request, and she doubled over with laughter. He thought surely she was not hearing right, so after she straightened up, he boldly, loudly, and clearly repeated that he wanted coconut-flavored ice cream.

The place exploded with laughter! Those around the tables heard what he emphasized, and some laughed so hard that they spewed ice cream onto the floor as they bent over in mirth! Others stared in silence at a dumb "Americano."

Knowing what the word looked like in Portuguese, Bennie pointed to the word on the list indicating available flavors of ice cream. Realizing he was the object of the hilarity, he clutched his brick of coconut ice cream and fled to the Jeep parked in front. With a roar and a spin of its wheels, he headed to a waiting wife and little daughter who would also delight in this delicious dessert.

Bennie had not grown up using street talk, and his language teachers with their etiquette had not mentioned such language in their lessons. By chance he discovered the correct meaning of the word he had used in the ice cream shop, when a worker digging a cesspool pointed to what Bennie had thought was the flavor of coconut ice cream! From then on, Bennie paid attention to having the accent in the right place and thanked God that he had not made that mistake in a church service trying to preach a sermon!

Preaching in Portuguese will be the next step, and soon, Bennie thought.

The idea thrilled and terrified him at the same time.

Robert and Jean Norris, founders of
Apostolic Bible Institute in Brazil

The reason for being a missionary:
"Jesus gave me the Holy Ghost!"

Great-tasting peacock bass

Faith in Him
Who Calleth

Bennie and Theresa had been in Manaus about fourteen months when they were ready to start their first church service in Portuguese. In a little more than a year, they had gained fluency in the language, finished the mission house, and, with funds provided by the First Pentecostal Church of Port Arthur, Texas, built a wooden church in a new suburb called Santo Antonio.

They celebrated Christmas Day 1966 by opening this church for services with a few curious neighbors and plenty of children attending. Many people came and went during the next few months but the DeMerchants continued preaching, teaching, and praying that God would give them souls. Bennie studied hard and prepared lessons to teach, and Theresa gathered children to listen to a Bible story and to sing to them as she played the accordion. She could go through anything, smiling even at times when Bennie got irritated at developing circumstances. Her nervous chuckle and listening ear won friendship almost instantly.

In the beginning as Bennie tried to preach in Portuguese, he often used the wrong word or verb tense. Smiles on the faces of his listeners clued him that he'd made a mistake. Theresa helped by writing any errors so that Bennie could study them and not repeat them. What he lacked in stating the correct verb tense or using the right adjective or noun, he made up in diligence. The people seemed to understand in spite of his shortcomings in the language, and at the close of one Sunday night church service, fourteen people came to the altar to repent.

In spite of the DeMerchants' faithful, hard work in the energy-sapping heat, they found it difficult to establish a work because people moved so often, always hoping that by relocating they could improve their fragile economic level. Many could pile all their personal belongings into the trunk of a taxi or into a bag on their backs.

They also found that, for Brazilians, attending church competed with two deeply rooted cultural forces: soccer and Carnival.

On their way to church on Sunday afternoons, Bennie and Theresa drove past a large soccer stadium about four blocks from the church. Thousands stood in line under a scorching sun to buy tickets to the game in the open stadium. The thermometer might read over 100 degrees in the shade, but the crowds would sit in the grandstands for three and four hours as their teams played soccer. Pele, their idol player, led the national team that won the world's championship cup three times. Soccer turned the people on like a master switch changing the laziest man into a fighting, running, cheering, screaming, flag-waving fan in pouring rain or 125-degree heat.

Bennie and Theresa, with blonde, blue-eyed Beth sometimes tucked into an oversized, thatch-woven shopping bag, her blue eyes and fair curls peeping out, traipsed up and down the streets of Santo Antonio, knocking on doors and inviting people to church. The hospitable Brazilians opened their doors to them and served them very strong coffee in tiny porcelain cups. As Bennie and Theresa slowly sipped the coffee-candy-tasting brew and conversed with them, many promised to come to church the next Sunday.

"Theresa, if 10 percent of those who promise to be at church for the next service attend, we will have to hang them from the wall," Bennie commented.

Alas, the next time Bennie met many of them, they were returning late in the afternoon from sitting on hard, backless seats under a broiling sun, watching a soccer game.

"Oh, sir," they would say, "it is too hot to come to church."

Brazilians also go wild over Carnival, a pre-Lent Catholic celebration that ends each year on Ash Wednesday, forty days before Easter. It is the largest and longest festival of fleshly, sensual activities that is promoted officially by taxpayers' money. Many schools, colleges, clubs, and other social organizations also sponsor carnivals in which all sorts of vices and revelry intensify to the weekend before Lent. Carnival and any special event are celebrated with much money being spent for fireworks and firecrackers in spite of their causing ear problems to bystanders who are too near when cannon-sounding fireworks explode too close to them.

A multitude of other religious holidays, festivals, and legal holidays during the year contribute to the low quality, slack efficiency, and meager production of the work force. In early days of ministry in Santo Antonio, Bennie and Theresa battled to evangelize these people under the sway of spiritualism and Catholicism. Many did not have even a form of godliness, much less any power. The work was growing painfully slowly over months of preaching and teaching to a number of adults, who at times could be counted on the fingers of one hand. Only a Holy Ghost revival would change their lives.

They held prayer meetings to pray for revival, but few attended. In one of these meetings, Bennie took off his glasses and put them ahead of his knees on the floor beneath the wooden pew. Later he discovered that someone had stolen these while he pled in prayer for souls.

Then one night Beth came down with a severe fever that continued all night. In spite of everything Bennie and Theresa did, Beth's temperature raged through her little body. Being the weekend, no doctors were in sight at any local, bureaucrat-laden hospital. Frustrated, Bennie held her in his arms under the Ladies' Auxiliary-furnished air conditioner of their room and prayed most of the night. Finally, Beth's temperature dropped, and Bennie slept. And had a reassuring dream.

He dreamed that he was in a church service with Brazilians. They were seated along rows of side galleries that were packed with their brown faces as far as he could see on both sides above the main floor. In this dream, he strode to the pulpit, opened his Bible, and preached to them from God's Word. It was an exhilarating service of worship and praise and victory!

On Sunday after this dream, he ministered with a revised attitude. He imagined that the handful of people represented this larger group that he saw in his dream. He would study, prepare, pray, and preach to them as if the pitiful number of people were a multitude.

As he preached, radios from the open houses around the church poured out the noise as the soccer game progressed. Everyone's radio blasted out his windows through the open ventilation areas at the top of the two sides of the church. Each time a team got a score, the roaring sound of "goooooooooooal" by the referee and fans sounded loud and long, continuing sometimes thirty seconds or longer as the radios blared and firecrackers exploded in the distance like a war had broken out.

Bennie hesitated until the noise calmed down, and continued preaching to his disoriented congregation as the cries of "goooooooooal" after "goooooooooal" roared through the neighborhood. Each time he looked at his congregation that he could fit into his car, they seemed lost in trying to understand what he was preaching to them because of the noise from the soccer stadium. A thought bludgeoned his mind like the rat-a-tat-tat of a jackhammer: *You might as well close your Bible, pack your bags, and go back to Canada while you are young! You will never have a church in this place. The people are all with me in the grandstands down here!*

He stubbornly rebuked that thought and kept on. Two months after they started church services in the Santo Antonio suburb, they put seven pews in their living room and opened the mission house in the central part of the city for meetings. Filled mostly with a few women and plenty of children, the closely compacted space had a cozy feeling that drew people. In a few months they moved the group from the living room to a two-car garage behind the mission house, thus doubling the space.

The work in the suburb also had grown to six or seven stable families who faithfully attended, and one by one God baptized them with the Holy Ghost.

In 1968 the DeMerchants ventured into the suburbs of Santa Luzia and São Francisco. This area in the strongholds of Satan abounded with much spiritism, and although the DeMerchants knocked on doors on street after street and held meetings for about one year, the only people who appeared were visitors who came with them in the van or walked from the central part of the city and already attended the house church.

After another unfruitful year of work in São Francisco, they closed up there also. Switching from unproductive areas after a reasonable effort would be part of their working strategy. Oh, how they needed good, well-trained, strong, challenging, and aggressive workers! They just couldn't take on Amazonas, or even Manaus, alone!

But neither could they stop trying. Bennie and Theresa translated lessons learned at the Apostolic Bible Institute. They had a manual Gestetner typewriter that they had purchased in 1964 and brought with them to Brazil. They ran cases and cases of paper through its rollers. Using English-Portuguese dictionaries, they laboriously translated the entire *Search for Truth* course, typed the Portuguese onto strips of white paper, and pasted the Portuguese translation over the English markings. Their weeks of work bore fruit as the Word took root. One woman received the Holy Ghost in the tank behind the mission house as Bennie baptized her. How they rejoiced! Things were starting to move. But the need for trained workers intensified.

During 1968 Bennie conducted two radio programs of half an hour on Sunday mornings, at seven and again at one in the afternoon. The DeMerchants realized they needed to move out of the garage church near downtown Manaus and look for something larger on a better and more permanent location. They prayed about this, but now in the middle of their first missionary term, it seemed the Missions Division struggled just to furnish them the bare basics with no extra funds available.

As the church grew and the message became more widely known through the radio programs, they found a few good men to train. Two or three other men embraced this great Oneness truth and were excitedly reading their Bibles as old passages became new with the illumination of the oneness of the Godhead in the person of Jesus Christ. They carried this doctrine to their friends and contacts whom they knew, before they were punished for joining such a "heretical" doctrine about Jesus and water baptism in His name.

On one occasion when another large evangelical church, which held strongly to the doctrine of the trinity, held a conference in Manaus with all its preachers and workers present from the interior, Bennie was surprised by a notable increase of inquiries by some of them when they came uninvited to his house. Dressed in suits, they appeared with Bibles in hand.

"We know that your church is new here and has a great future," some remarked after a handshake and small talk. "We have heard that you need experienced ministers to work with you to evangelize the Amazon state! We would like to help you do this."

Their inquiry seemed reasonable. But eventually they would come around to the final question, "What kind of salaries do you have set up for your ministers and other benefits to their wives and families while they preach?"

Bennie had read the book, *The Indigenous Church*, by Melvin Hodges and knew that if workers appeared from another church who wanted a monthly guaranteed amount of support, their work and loyalty would last as long as the check or until they had a bigger offer elsewhere.

One day another of these ministers appeared at the door with the same questions.

Finally Bennie asked, "Why are many workers and ministers from this other large church that has been working for several decades in this area suddenly interested in working with us?"

He was answered immediately: "At our convention we have been discussing the doctrine of your church at length and the reason it is beginning to grow. We decided that the North Americans were backing this young Canadian missionary, and he was paying salaries to anyone who would be baptized into the church and help preach this erroneous doctrine anywhere."

With this false information presented as a reason to their convention, Bennie understood why he was getting so many offers from their ministers wanting to work with him! But the DeMerchants were soon to get the kind of help they desperately needed.

Halfway through June 1968, two friends of long standing visited Bennie and Theresa. With delight the missionaries welcomed Sister Margaret Calhoun and Sue Pippin, a roommate of Theresa's from ABI. Both attended the church in Madison, Wisconsin, pastored by Brother Jack Yonts. Sister Margaret had two loves: children and missions. She loved to teach and had studied diligently to acquire her master's degree in elementary education.

Sister Margaret, Sue, Theresa, and Bennie flew on an old Catalina amphibious aircraft two hundred miles west to the interior town of Coari. After spending the night in a local hotel, they returned by an Amazon River passenger boat to

Manaus. As usual, the boat stopped at many small towns, taking on passengers and jungle farm products and arriving a day and a half later in Manaus. Sister Margaret was very impressed with the encounter with people.

"This is exactly the place I want to work," she told the DeMerchants. "Here and with the children who crowd into the garage services. Brother Bennie, will you recommend me to Brother Vouga as a missionary teacher?"

Would he! Bennie and Theresa could hardly breathe for a few minutes. To have help! And such help as Sister Margaret could give! Oh, joy! Oh, *joy*!

Sister Margaret not only petitioned the FMD to be allowed to go to Manaus as a missionary teacher, she received her appointment the fall of 1968 and began to deputize through the Midwest. Besides her travel expenses, she raised about three thousand dollars that was sent to FMD.

Meanwhile, the DeMerchants' efforts to reach the native people plowed ahead. The Manaus church had stabilized into a solid core of believers in the Santo Antonio suburb and downtown in the garage behind the DeMerchants' residence.

Then, as the end of 1968 approached, Theresa received a letter from her mother that Theresa's dad had suffered a stroke and wasn't expected to live.

"Theresa, come home to Wisconsin if you want to see your dad while he yet lives," she urged.

The young couple had no emergency funds, but Bennie's mother knew about the situation and said she would supply money for Theresa's ticket if necessary.

Theresa didn't know what to do. Telephone connections proved impossible. She prayed and opened her Bible to II Timothy 4:9, "Do thy diligence to come shortly unto me." What a direct answer!

Theresa was expecting their second child and had no maternity clothes for cold weather. She borrowed a winter coat from another missionary and flew home. Wanting to surprise Brother Shomberg, Theresa's mother did not tell him Theresa was coming. When Theresa arrived in the hospital room, her father thought he was still delirious and couldn't believe she really arrived. When she returned the next day, he accepted her for real and thanked the Lord. From then on, his condition improved.

Sister Margaret bought Theresa a warm maternity dress for the trip. The next weekend, Theresa received a call from Eleanor Grant. Brother S. G. Norris wanted her to speak at church Sunday night! She had worked and taught at ABI for five years after her graduation, so that was home also. She did her best to relate God's blessings on Brazil. She also mentioned that they held services in their garage and needed some land for a central church. The Lord blessed in a great way, and in that service the people gave a special offering of $2,000 for a lot.

The following week, when Theresa arrived back in Manaus, she found no food in the cupboard. Bennie had been praying and fasting for four days for some land. And Theresa had the $2,000 check in her hand during all those four days!

Bennie sent the check to headquarters in Saint Louis until they could locate a good lot. Then one day as they were passing out tracts on Castelo Branco Avenue, they met a lady who insisted that they buy her land for their church. This lot at 697 President Castelo Branco Avenue was about a long block from their home nearby on Ramos Ferreira Street. What a fantastically convenient location! They bought the land for about $4,000, using the $2,000 check and money from other personal deals Bennie was able to negotiate.

Their second daughter, Pamela Bea, was born April 8, 1969, in Manaus. Theresa cut the long sleeves off Ben's shirts and fashioned them into baby gowns for the new little mite. Right afterward, Brother Sam Baker had an emergency and phoned for Ben to fly to São Paulo, some 2,500 miles south. The phones were poor communication and they had no idea about the problem, but Ben tried to be obedient to their Brazilian overseer, so they bought a ticket on credit.

Theresa was left alone with Beth and the new baby. No formula agreed with Pam's fragile system, and she lost weight rapidly. Seeking help, Theresa walked the streets in the relentless sun, carrying her five-pound bundle and shepherding Beth. The doctor prescribed several formulas, but nothing worked. People on the street would look at Theresa and say, "Look at that tiny baby."

Theresa prayed at night and pleaded, "Lord, don't let my baby die." Tears dripping down her cheeks, she cradled Pam and sang, "Jesus Loves Me." Then inspiration struck: She would look for an evaporated milk like Carnation, called Ideal. The next day she trudged from store to store until she found some Ideal milk. Thankfully, Pamela did well on that. Thank God for good ideas!

The DeMerchants were rapidly coming to the end of their first term on the field. They announced in their newsletters of their intention to build a central church on the recently purchased lot on the avenue. Slowly funds earmarked for the building trickled into mission headquarters.

Bennie wanted to get the shell of the central church building up and covered before they finished their first term, but building funds were limited and they needed to stretch every dollar as far as possible. He had built a house and knew that plastering and finish work cost a lot in materials and labor. But what if he could devise a block that negated the necessity of plastering? Bennie put his ingenuity to work:

I wanted to make a type of cement block that could be fabricated from a simple portable form that would take the place of four of the largest clay bricks and would be smooth on each side, requiring no plastering. I worked with two men for three days with sand and a bag of cement trying to make something that could easily come out of the form and that could be made on the construction site. We succeeded in making the desired form, and we also came up with a large waffle-like form that could be put in the same walls in place of windows. This cut down on wooden window frames or iron works and eliminated a lot of the building costs.

They created two forms that were the same size, for wall blocks that weighed about forty-four pounds each. The blocks could be made on a smooth floor surface on a sheet of plastic, and each worker could make about 100 square feet of wall blocks or 80 square feet of window-lattice blocks per day. In thirty hours of hardening and drying time, the blocks could be placed into the walls. They would not need plastering nor painting but could be washed with a water hose and wire brush to preserve their smooth, natural cement color. If they were carefully sealed using white tile cement for joints and the joints smoothed by passing round plastic pipe along their grooves, the blocks looked neat with the white joints for contrast.

Wood that can resist rot and termites in the Amazon only lasts about ten years. The solid blocks and lattice window blocks could be built cheaply using local labor, so this construction method in northern Brazil caught hold. It has been used to erect about eighty-seven churches since 1968.

A great work was slowly being put together that would stabilize local churches with a place to meet and establish permanence. Step by step the One who called Bennie and Theresa was leading them over many obstacles of the beginnings of a new work on the mission field.

Faithful is He who calleth you. He will do it!

And, as Bennie and Theresa were about to discover, He would do it more abundantly above all they could ask or think.

The
Denuded Rooster

In their third year of ministry in Manaus, Bennie and Theresa decided to take the advice of the evangelical minister who told them to "take your message to the jungle." They started to follow leads to jungle river towns and areas where preaching opportunities beckoned.

The first road built out of Manaus connected them to Manacapuru, a town about fifty-five miles west, located at a sweeping turn of the Amazon River. Brother Manuel Bizerra, whom Bennie had baptized in a jungle creek in Manaus, started house meetings there and asked them to visit and to baptize the new believers.

To Manacapuru from Manaus on a passenger boat on the Amazon took a whole day. That time could be cut to half a day when the mud road opened and travelers were able to ride the wood-framed bus built on a truck chassis. Bennie opted for the bus and bought a ticket for a numbered seat. When he climbed aboard, he discovered that a woman and her lap full of little ones had preempted his place. Fellow passengers occupied all the other seats. The bus had oversold its capacity on that busy weekend and planned to put some of the passengers on top of the bus.

Rather than complain to the driver, Bennie obligingly climbed up the ladder on the side of the bus to the baggage area on its roof, where a small platform with rails on each side held the baggage and excess passengers. The vehicle, overloaded and top-heavy, swayed alarmingly at times. Along the road on some areas, it became mired in mud. All hands got out to help push it through the mud holes, but, though sunburnt, Bennie made it to Manacapuru in time for the evening service. He quickly realized a strong work was going to develop in this first jungle town outside Manaus on the Amazon River.

Brother Manuel at Manacapuru had a large family, and though they had a small jungle plot on which to raise vegetables, he complained about the difficulties in getting food at the local market.

Bennie had already discovered a type of peacock bass the local folk called *tucunare*. He had no interest in the type of fish offered in the markets. They looked like scavengers or were slimy, scaleless, bottom-feeding fish with long whiskers. Peacock bass, however, are a top-notch eating fish and one of the highest priced in the market.

The natives caught tucunare with a heavy nylon line on a hook baited with a live minnow. They held the line in their hands from a boat stopped or tied to a bush. Sometimes the natives would use a shiny, four-inch lure that they swung around and around on a line over their head, released it to splash into the lake, and pulled in the line hand over hand while the lure's action attracted a tucunare.

The idea of fly-fishing for tucunare was unheard of. Having neither brought a fishing rod to the field nor seen a fly rod in a local store, Bennie earlier had his brother in Canada send him a rod and some streamer flies by parcel post. Under the right conditions, in the early morning when the sun was low, the water dropping, and near a full or new moon, the flies worked.

"Brother Manuel," Bennie declared, "you do not have to worry about buying fish at the local market when you and your family live and pastor this church in front of this dark water of the lake! You can catch tucunares right out there!"

After preaching that night, Bennie stayed with the pastor. Early the next morning, he swung out of his hammock and sent Brother Manuel's son to the corner store.

"Bring me back some fishhooks as long as my finger," he instructed the lad, tossing him a few coins.

With the fishhooks, Bennie proceeded to show the pastor how to make a fly that would catch fish. He borrowed a five-position long-handled pair of pliers to use for a vise, black nylon thread from Brother Manuel's wife, and a pair of house scissors. He spotted among the chickens a nice, red-necked rooster.

"Please bring that rooster to me," he requested. After they did so, he snitched a few long red hackles from its neck.

"Now scratch your dog," he said. While the animal relaxed, Bennie cut some long black hairs from its tail and some white hair from its belly.

By then a crowd of onlookers had gathered. Bennie was in business for setting up his fly-tying shop on the Amazon. The circle of people around him watched as he inserted the curl of his hook into the pliers and straightened its offset shank. He wound the base of this famous fly with the black nylon thread while the pastor's boy held it tightly in the pliers. Next he placed white hair on the bottom of the hook and the dark on top and tied it off with a knot in the thread. Then he proceeded to tie on the red rooster's hackle tip and wind it around the hook three times as the onlookers watched it fuzz out in the sunlight. He built up the hook's head with black thread, tying a knot in it several times. Using clear fingernail polish, he painted the head of the hook to protect the nylon thread from the tightening leader knot. As the fly-tying lesson ended, Bennie saw smiles and comments of what the "Americano" could do with nothing.

"This fly hook will catch peacock bass if you troll it by hand in a jerky motion to imitate a minnow swimming," he explained. "You can make your own flies that will work when you fish from canoes as you paddle them slowly."

Over a month later, he caught the old wood-bodied bus and went to preach and spend the night in Manacapuru. The work was growing, and the little church was filling up. Upon Bennie's arrival, the worker told him that the "Americano" *did* know something about fishing for peacock bass.

Ever since he showed them how to make simple artificial flies, they had been catching tucunares, not needing to buy any fish at the local market.

After getting out of his hammock early the next morning to have devotions and coffee with Brother Manuel and his family, Bennie decided to go to the water tap on the back of the house to lather his face and shave. While scraping his beard, he watched their daughter as she tossed dried corn to the chickens in the back yard. Except for one loner that stayed at a safe distance, all the chickens flocked to her to eat it off the ground.

"Is that chicken sick?" Bennie asked the child.

"It's all right," she replied, "but it won't come near the ground corn until everyone goes inside the house and closes the door."

The rooster was indeed a sickly looking critter. His neck had been stripped bare.

"Why, this is the old bird that I snipped the hackles from a month ago to show you how to make streamer flies for peacock bass!" Bennie exclaimed, realizing that the natives had denuded the creature to make flies for fishing and selling.

Beyond Manacapuru no roads penetrated the jungle. Bennie's only recourse for reaching towns and villages along the Amazon was to endure trips that seemed like an eternity. The boat chugged along in the blanketing heat with its hull slowly plowing against the Amazon's muddy current. Boat captains always overloaded their boats to squeeze as much profit as possible from each trip. Crowded together like sardines in a can, people slept aboard on hammocks strung across the upper and lower wooden decks. As the boat turned, the wind would often blow the black diesel-engine exhaust fumes in their faces and leave their clothes and hammocks black with soot. Passengers coughed and waited for the boat to traverse a bend in the river, change course, and hopefully spew the exhaust in another direction.

In the rainy season it could rain all day or on and off. Showers often soaked the passengers on one side where the canvas awnings could not be lowered or secured from the strong wind. Every half-hour or less the boat would stop at a jungle farm to load more stalks of green bananas, tropical fruit, pigs, chickens, ducks and maybe a few more passengers. Then the waterline would creep up a few inches closer to the top of the wooden hull. Every few months newspaper headlines blazed out the sad tale of boat disasters where overloaded passenger boats on the Amazon or one of its tributaries struck a nearly immersed log, puncturing the boat's plank hull or hitting another boat in fog. In some cases more than one hundred people drowned as the boat sank helplessly in the night.

Such trips were time consuming even when the boats ran on schedule, but in such loaded conditions the heavy, hardwood-hulled boats wallowed against the current. The heat of the daytime sun and the clouds of mosquitoes that billowed from the floating grass on the shore at night caused any comfort to flee. With pieces of baggage and belongings on board, a passenger hardly dared to take his eyes off these items due to thieves and pilferers.

On long trips the traveler had to take his own safe drinking water in large thermos jugs packed full of ice or drink the boat's water filtered from the Amazon River. When there was no filter system on board, rather than drink water directly from the Amazon, as many did, Bennie purchased a ripe watermelon from a stop at a local farm. Once after having eaten a good part of this natural water source and joining the watermelon halves to avoid evaporation, he spent a couple of hours in the hammock. Thirsty, he separated the watermelon he had cut earlier. Only the hollow rinds were left!

Much of the food served on board the riverboat was dried, salted fish, re-soaked, cooked, served, and eaten with the main staple of the area, manioc meal or rice. Sometimes locals purchased fresh fish on the trip for serving passengers on board several days. Long lines of people usually waited at mealtime in a limited table-and-bench area near the rear of the boat. After seeing the meal being prepared in the rear kitchen mess area, Bennie preferred to start a fast.

Bennie had made several trips and became frustrated with boats whose owners would change schedules if they thought cargo arriving a day later would bring more money. Bennie did not want to waste his time on these overloaded boats. He had walked from stem to stern or dodged under the edges of hammocks and watched the muddy water and the jungle slip slowly by for days as he used the only means to get to the Amazon's larger jungle towns.

Bennie had previously joined the local Aero-club on Flores airstrip north of the city, and had taken the written tests in Portuguese at the larger airport when their Department of Aeronautics examiners came from Rio de Janeiro. Based on the written Portuguese test, Brazilian medical exam, his foreign pilot license, and his being a permanent resident, Bennie acquired a Brazilian pilot's license. A local businessman of Italian descent, Italo Bianco, loved to fly and was president of the Aero-club. He bought a Cessna 172 aircraft on wheels but did not have his license. Bennie instructed the man until the fellow soloed and later acquired his own private pilot license. In this way Bennie had kept his flying skills legally current.

Sometime in the future our work will have to switch gears for transportation needs, Bennie thought. *The two-thousand-mile-wide Amazon Basin in northern Brazil is one huge, overwhelming, roadless jungle. To reach these people by road is impossible, and to reach them by boat is interminable. But if I had a floatplane ... .*

Flying
a Turtle

On May 20, 1970, the DeMerchants left Brazil
for their first furlough after four and one-half years
on the field. Amid hard work, setbacks, and
frustrations, victories had blossomed. A permanent
church housing the Manaus congregation had been
built, and the jungle outreach church in Manacapuru
had stabilized. In addition, two other preaching
points promised great potential.

Sister Margaret had arrived in Manaus by
Booth Steamship lines from New Orleans in early
September 1969. The DeMerchants had already built
a small apartment for her above their house, using
funds Sister Margaret had raised. The Ladies'
Ministries in the United States furnished the place
with air conditioner, stove, and refrigerator. Sheaves
For Christ had purchased a new, beige Volkswagen
Bug for her. Sister Margaret dedicated her time to
studying Portuguese and attending local church

services or accompanying Theresa in evangelism, visiting homes, leaving tracts, and inviting people to church.

Before they left on furlough, Bennie and Theresa transferred to her some of the work responsibility of the four new churches with about 125 members and five or six workers. A young Portuguese Brazilian business couple rented the DeMerchants' downstairs furnished home, giving Sister Margaret some protection by their presence inside the high bricked walls with barbed wire on top.

A good evangelist from São Paulo who had a lot of experience and zeal also helped in Manaus. He would take Sister Margaret with her accordion and other workers and have meetings on the street. In one of these services a young man, Jonas Siqueira, received a tract.

Jonas had come from Autazes, a small town in the jungle about seventy-five miles southeast of Manaus. He was visiting his mother, who was dying with cancer in a hospital in the city and asked for prayer. His mother died, but he soon became a firm believer, hard worker, and long-lasting friend. Sister Margaret went with the others on the twenty-four-hour boat trip to his town and held meetings on the streets. Dozens were baptized. Unfortunately, having no place to go for meetings and no trained worker living in the town, many of the new converts became disorientated and melted into other religious groups or quit.

Contacts with people from the small work in Manacapuru segued into house meetings, and many received the baptism of the Holy Ghost on a nine-mile-long island in the Amazon River above this town. All the houses were built on stilts about five or six feet above the ground, and when the river rose from heavy rains, water swirled all around the houses, the current carrying huge balls of floating grass down the Amazon River. This would last a month or more as the river, at its peak, isolated homeowners in their homes with water running underneath.

Many families who lived on this island above Manacapuru had come from the Tarauacá and the upper Juruá River area, where they previously worked tapping rubber trees. When a family broke away and arrived closer to the city, they found free land on the frequently flooded islands and built their houses on them. Some of these islands were only eight or ten miles long with hundreds of people living there and growing jute. Once a family arrived and sent back word that they had their own land, others moved down the following year. Though poor, the people were serious and hard workers.

Sister Margaret loved to go to such places with a flannelboard and tell Bible stories to small children. She would make the stories simple, but her audience would grow considerably by large numbers of adults who devoured everything she said. In the evening services, a worker would preach, and soon these places would need a church building. These numerous lowland islands in the Amazon River systems were fertile ground for preaching the gospel.

When the DeMerchants left Manaus for furlough, they went as passengers on a DC-3, a twin-engine propeller plane, to the border of Brazil near Colombia, stopping on the crooked Juruá River in Carauarí for refueling. As Bennie looked at this convoluted river from the air, he wondered how long it would take him to reach into these areas made at least five times distant due to its winding course.

When they reached Miami, Brother Wayne Rooks, a member of the Foreign Missionary Board, met them and helped them to find a good, used white Chevrolet car. A pleasant surprise greeted them in Saint Louis when they were introduced to the new Faith Promise plan and the Partners In Missions program. Instead of zigzagging across the country making their own contacts and schedules, they would now be working with District Foreign Missions representatives, who would streamline their travel agenda.

With help from Brother Paul Box, the Foreign Missions secretary, the DeMerchants drew up a basic monthly operational budget for their field and its needs for the next term. Bennie presented to the Administrative Committee a request for approval to raise funds for five church buildings in the Amazon that had become a district of the United Pentecostal Church of Brazil. He also projected their goals for the next term.

"We hope that at some time in the future we could acquire a seaplane to visit these areas in quick, efficient visits as the work grows," Bennie's report stated.

After two days in Saint Louis, they drove to Wisconsin to visit Theresa's family, by now diminished by the loss of her father. Several days later, they journeyed to New Brunswick. Both places warmed their hearts with enthusiastic welcomes.

In New Brunswick, Bennie and a friend drove to the Miramichi River near upper Blackville to fish for Atlantic salmon. Bennie had hardly waded into the river with his fly rod when someone high on the bank hollered for him to come to the phone.

His heart beating furiously, Bennie thought, *Something must have happened! Who would bother to call me way out here?*

"Bennie, you'd better sit down," a voice advised him. Bennie struggled to swallow the lump that had formed in his throat. *What has happened?* he wondered. *Has something happened to Theresa? the girls?*

"Brother DeMerchant, there has been a settlement on the hull insurance of the mission's aircraft accident in Liberia, West Africa," the voice continued. "The United Pentecostal Church decided not to replace this aircraft at this time. It has been decided to apply this check of $10,000 toward the purchase of a floatplane for Brazil."

What a phone call!

On September 25, 1970, the DeMerchants returned to Saint Paul, Minnesota. Gerald Grant had worked with the Foreign Missions Division to purchase a Cessna 172 seaplane that had only two hundred hours' flying time since factory. This all-metal plane was STOL (Short Take-Off and Landing) with long wing flange and drooping wing tips. The ex-owner had upgraded to a larger seaplane and left this one for sale at $13,000. The Foreign Missions Division advanced the extra $3,000 to purchase it, providing Bennie would travel throughout the winter and raise the difference, the extra cost of the pontoons.

During the next seven months the DeMerchant family raised Partners In Missions commitments in the United States and Canada for their next term on the field. By the end of April 1971, the Cessna 172 had passed a tight export inspection and was ready to be ferried to its new base in Manaus, Brazil.

Bennie had arranged for an instrument-rated Pentecostal flight instructor, David Wright, to fly with him to Manaus. Flying a floatplane was quite different from Bennie's experience and limitations, and having Wright aboard would greatly enhance Bennie's safety on the trip. The two met at Greenville Lake in Illinois, where Bennie practiced takeoffs and landings on the water until dwellers called the police, who ran them off to the next lake. They flew in early to Lake Carlyle, refueled for the next leg of the flight south, and waited there for the dedication service of the seaplane.

The secretary of Foreign Missions, Brother Box, wanted to dedicate this Cessna 172 seaplane. So on May 11, General Superintendent Stanley Chambers spoke at this seaplane dedication at Carlyle Lake in Illinois. Brother Chambers claimed that he had not found any precedent in Scripture for dedicating a seaplane but finally settled on I Corinthians 9:22, "That I might by all means save some."

"This seaplane," Chambers predicted, "will be the means of reaching many in the huge Amazon

River system, and Brother DeMerchant is taking it to Brazil for that purpose."

After the message, all present went to the water's edge and put their hands on some part of the seaplane during the dedicatory prayer. Little did they know that this seemingly feeble seaplane, witnessed as being so weak by so many, would fly tens of thousands of takeoffs, wear out nine new or overhauled engines in the next thirty-five years, and take His workers to all kinds of people in the world's largest standing forest, the "lungs of the world."

Bennie was the ripe old age of twenty-nine and had not yet acquired a low, gravelly flight captain's voice, but he had logged 328 hours of flight experience since his first solo. It was only a fifty-nine-hour flight in a Cessna 172 seaplane from Lake Elmo near Saint Paul, Minnesota, to Rio Negro's dark waters in front of Manaus, Brazil. The distance could normally be flown in twelve days or in eight if in a hurry. It took Bennie forty-seven days, and during that time just about everything that could go wrong did.

All went well until the two men reached South Caicos Island. At this island, the engine gradually lost power and would not even idle. Though they were nestled in a sheltered cove, the wind blew them backward and out to the high seas with huge waves.

Bennie flipped on the radio. "Control tower, please phone the harbor and get someone with a boat to come out quickly and tow us back in!"

During the eternity before the boat arrived, Bennie stepped onto the pontoon and paddled furiously, but against the wind he barely held the plane in place. The water grew deeper and rougher before the boat finally arrived and towed the seaplane back to the moored starting point. They charged Bennie and Dave a stiff fee for the rescue!

What frustration! The two men spent seven days at Admiral's Arms Hotel. With a plane mechanic at the hotel who was flying through, they checked the fuel, ignition, and all. The engine refused to run on its very low compression. They had no tools. The battery was flat.

Aggravated that the only resident aircraft mechanic was drunk all week, they watched the number of their traveler's checks diminish as they paid their bills for food and lodging. They waited five days for headquarters to get them a telegram acknowledging their position and giving permission to do whatever was necessary to continue. From this, Bennie learned—and learned it well—that when you're out in the boonies, you have to solve your problems as best as you can and report later. It was a situation for prayer, and pray they did.

Finally another floatplane going north came from Grenada with a load of people on board. The Canadian pilot helped Bennie and Dave empty their fuel into the Canadian plane. Then they pulled the empty seaplane onto a beach so covered with seashells that it would not hold any pegs for tie-downs. After heading the plane into the general direction of the trade wind, the men carried seawater and filled each compartment of the floats, making the plane so heavy that it would not be blown away while they were gone.

The kind Canadian pilot also helped them dismount their engine. He flew it with his load to

Miami the same day while Bennie and Dave jumped on an old DC-3 cargo plane. When Wright arrived in Miami, he sent the engine to Houston, Texas, to an overhaul shop. Bennie bought a seat on an airliner to Manaus where, without word from the long overdue seaplane, Theresa and others had grown concerned.

A month later Bennie flew to Houston to retrieve the newly overhauled engine. With pilot Mark Holiday, Bennie returned to South Caicos Island, installed the engine on the beach, and test-flew the plane before heading south to Brazil. Alone.

On June 16, 1971, with only three hours on the engine after the major overhaul, Bennie took off from South Caicos Island for San Juan, Puerto Rico. Once this island dropped from view, Bennie flew over the ocean in headwinds for an hour and twenty minutes. Then he realized that circumstance played in his favor and this aircraft engine's failure happened in the best possible part of the trip. Had he lost power over the open ocean, at best he would have lost the little bird. Now he would arrive in Brazil with this new engine.

Saint Thomas, then Saint Croix passed beneath the wings. At Guadalupe, Bennie touched down and waited for customs and immigration to come in a small harbor boat after his international flight to welcome him to their island. After what seemed a long time dealing with customs, immigration, papers, and drug police searches, he was finally released. His arrival was extraordinary. He was a Canadian citizen with an American-owned aircraft and a permanent residence card for Brazil!

Early the next morning, he taxied in the calm, salty waters of this French island's harbor with confidence. He'd had a refreshing sleep. A new day lay ahead. The weather looked great. The well-fueled plane sported a new engine. He was now closer to Manaus. In the air he would activate his international flight plan to Georgetown, Guiana, and finally make the South American coast.

Before long his little bird was soaring along the Venezuela-Guiana coast with lowland tropical vegetation on his right side and the blue Atlantic Ocean on the left. But as the plane trundled farther south, the weather turned sour and dropped lower and lower. Black clouds materialized from nowhere and enveloped everything, the wind began to juggle the plane, and rain pelted down. He dropped to one hundred feet above the waves and kept an eye on the coastline with its tropical vegetation.

The plane bounced and slewed sideways in jaw-jarring rainy gusts while he flew closer and closer to the coast. With no forward visibility, intense turbulence, pouring rain, and weak side visibility, he decided to sit in one of the many coastal inlets offering shelter.

Thank God I am on floats and can tie up to a bush in this sheltered water and wait out this weather, he mused. *I just hope no big 'gator mistakes my white pontoon for one of his watery friends.*

After about an hour of waiting through tropical torrents and electrical welding works, Bennie took off for Georgetown. He later learned from other pilots that the leg of the flight along the northeastern South American coast has produced the greatest numbers of visual pilots who decided to quit flying if their names had not already been mentioned in obituaries.

He crossed Venezuela and entered the Amazon watershed, where he touched down at Boa Vista, the capital of Roraima state, Brazil. *Little bird, you will contribute to helping this city be connected by road to the rest of Brazil,* Bennie promised.

Two days later, June 22, the Edo 2000 pontoons of this "Gospel Duck" splashed on the water in front of São Raimundo, a suburb on the waterfront of Manaus, and taxied to the veranda of the Araujos, a church member's home.

Then the fun began.

Gerald and Eleanor Grant

In the beginning there was a 'lil church in
Manacapuru—today Jerusalem II

2008 - UPC of Brazil congregation at Jerusalem II
in Manacapuru, Amazonas, Brazil

The Mission Takes Wing

Bennie was now in his early thirties and raring to go. Sheaves For Christ had helped him to get a piece of equipment to reach the Amazon, an area in Brazil equal to all the land east of the Mississippi River. Opportunities to move into cities and towns along the river poured in from every side. With much work, flying, ministering, and using everyone they could trust, by the help of God and the prayers of God's people, the DeMerchants moved ahead. Sometimes Bennie felt as if he were walking on air. Each move they made seemed to produce a harvest of souls.

The suburbs around Manaus expanded as people came and pushed back the jungle around this huge metropolis. It was not unreal to hear of someone killing a wild jaguar less than ten miles from this jungle-enclosed city. But settlers expanded to a second and third hill or more and built suburbs called Coroado I, II, and III, Alvorada, Cidade Nova, João Paula, Compensa, Lírio do Vale, Santo Augustinho, etc. As the suburbs expanded, so did the church with new congregations that needed buildings in which to meet and worship.

Men from the local churches in the city made cement blocks at their simple brick factory in Coroado, a Manaus suburb. Some of the men became so skilled in making cement blocks and ventilated wall tile that the blocks looked like they came from a more complicated factory with brick-forming equipment. The blocks, weighing forty-five to forty-eight pounds each, were then hauled in the church-owned truck to the building sites of the dozens of local churches.

However, nothing moves on Brazilian roads without a bill of sale that guarantees that a 17 percent tax was paid when material changed hands. Once an inspector stopped Bennie on the highway.

"Your bill of sale from where you purchased the blocks, Sir," he demanded.

Bennie explained that they were made on their church property, with sand cement purchased with an already taxed bill of sale. "I am general pastor of the church and driving the church-owned truck to another one of our churches," he continued. "The taxed water from the church water bill we pay each month for them to pump from the Amazon was the final ingredient that went into the blocks."

The inspector was not convinced. Something had to be wrong if taxes were not being paid on top of taxes already charged. Frustrated that there was no change of hands or further taxes to be paid, the officer seized the truck and called Bennie to their headquarters. They wanted an extra 25 percent industrial tax on the finished product, or they would also seize the equipment at the church's "cement block plant."

Bennie waited while another officer went to check this out and only found a wooden form worth about five bucks when new. But to get the truck back he had to pay the estimated value of tax on that load. That episode quickly taught him to avoid paying the "industrial tax." From then on, they just took the inexpensive, lightweight forms by truck or airplane to the new location, where they made their own materials for church buildings, thus using donated labor as much as possible and without breaking any law.

As the work grew in new towns and cities out of Manaus, the floatplane came at the right time. No road connected this city in the heart of the rain forest with southern Brazil. The river was the highway that boats and barges navigated with passengers and freight. As a rule of thumb, a minute in the seaplane took an hour by boat. The airplane crossed in a second or two some narrow necks of land between turns of the river that by boat or barge would take hours. It was boring, tiresome, and fuel expending to travel as a boat passenger on the Juruá, Purus, Javarí, Jutaí, and upper Madeira Rivers and some of their tributaries.

In those early years, maps drawn up in the 1940s during World War II were Bennie's source of flight information. They were generally correct in basic information but weak on details and marked heavily with "terrain data unknown." As he flew into new areas, he soon learned not to depend on those old World Aeronautical Charts (WACs). Some towns were twenty-five or more miles off their position shown on the maps.

If in doubt of his location and gallons of fuel counted, Bennie always landed on sight of the first sign of civilization. Some dwellings were abandoned or seasonally occupied. One or more canoes tied up at the river's edge indicated the presence of people who waved or ran when he circled overhead. Often when he landed and water-taxied back to their canoe on shore, every person had fled to the woods. Peeking from the shade, they watched a Canadian exclaim in their language that all was well and he was Pastor Bennie, who was seeking information and needed directions, a nice way to avoid saying he was lost.

Slowly the older men (or man), sometimes with old, three-piece shotguns, would slowly walk down the path from the jungle behind their homes, trailing other family members. They were afraid. They never had an airplane land on the river in front of their homes.

"How many beaches to _____?" Bennie would ask.

Local folks born on these crooked rivers often did not know the river more than a few turns above or below them. Their world is very small. They measure distance in those rivers by *prias* or beaches up or down the river to a certain place. In the dry season, each switchback river with low water leaves sand beaches or mud banks. As the river recedes to its lowest level, the beaches get longer and more shallow-angled to the water. The river dwellers counted beaches up or down the river as they made their trips.

The comparison of the seaplane to boat travel time has its extremes. A local businessman in Eirunepé on the Juruá River told Bennie he opened a jungle farm at the headwaters of the Jutaí River over the divide between these rivers just north of town. From where the Jeep stopped, they went on foot through jungle to a waiting canoe on the Jutaí, carrying what they could in the heat. But when the man wanted to send heavier equipment for sawing logs, generators, and cement by boat to this location, it took six months in low water. Imagine his delight when fifteen minutes after full throttle on Juruá with the seaplane, Bennie was easing down on one pontoon in a turn on the narrow Jutaí in front of his jungle farmhouse, ready for coffee!

The seaplane could carry cement block forms and some sheet metal for roofs in its belly, but sometimes to obtain a church building, Bennie needed only its wings. In the early revival in Maués, large numbers in the town believed and came to God. Opposition ran strong. The building in which folks gathered for services had been rented for short periods by other groups, and they were not happy at all to see the DeMerchants' progress. Due to property complications, the businessman who owned it lived in Manaus and wanted to sell this building. Bennie learned that the other group wanted to purchase the building to block his acquiring it. The other party sent a negotiator to Manaus to buy it from the owner.

With the aid of the seaplane, Bennie arrived several hours before the competition.

"What is your price for that building in Maués?" Bennie asked the owner.

When the owner quoted a reasonable figure, Bennie agreed to the deal. An hour later the two men left the recording office in Manaus with Bennie clutching the initial papers in hand for that property deed. Hours later the other group discovered what Bennie had done.

Many sister congregations were birthed out of Maués. Once Bennie baptized seventy-three people in the same day. The churches nearby had several large families and worked hard. They made their simple churches from palm thatch roofs with poles for the sides, or, if able, they bought boards from local sawmills or used flattened, thick bark from trees to nail on these poles to cover the space. Glass pop bottles, with their caps punched to allow a wick to be twisted and pulled through, were filled with kerosene for lamps to provide light. Small poles about the size of a man's wrist, when split into four open splinters on top, held the bottles snugly.

Early in the work Bennie and Theresa established a lifelong bond with these people. Although hardworking and industrious, at times they were unable in heavy rainy season and floods to feed their families properly. At such times Bennie would drop in from the sky in various places with a plane totally loaded with food stuff and boxes of used clothing their North American friends sent them. (The UPCI in Brazil has assistance and tax exemption status for postal reception and not by air freight or airlines.) At other times, Bennie ferried in doctors, nurses, and medicine to vaccinate and consult with the natives, their children, and the babies. Many times he wished he were a doctor!

The Brazilians knew the DeMerchants were not God or Santa Claus but were in that country to preach the gospel, show them how to work, tithe, and support their own ministers. Many trained workers rose to the challenge to reach those in rural areas, villages, towns, cities, and the capitals of this huge "inland sea." Accepting the gospel brought a positive change to them, their living conditions, and educational level. The simple preaching and teaching of the gospel worked. But even with an airplane, Bennie and Theresa were overloaded with work. How badly they needed many more trained men!

The DeMerchants demanded much from the workers they did have. They all knew what each other was doing and copied each other, helped each other, and prayed for each other as they moved ahead. The workers felt the DeMerchants' confidence and trust. God blessed them.

After the first five years or so, Bennie refused to baptize the converts of the workers, lest the people think he always had to be around. He wanted them to preach and to teach others to do so. Training and moving out were the keys. It was a period of fast moving around.

"How do you erect a church building where the people are so poor?" Bennie was often asked. He explained:

The workers would acquire a lot from city hall that got behind on taxes. Seeking votes, the mayor arranged for the lot to be sold cheaply to us. Cement sent earlier, a month or more, on a barge coming up a crooked river against the current and dry season shoals had arrived. We only needed water and sand, both in abundance in the area, and we were ready to mix these two with cement and go to work. In the dry season, many huge beaches would appear on river turns, so our church people would get a large, empty boat hull and with their bucket brigade load the boat with sand and tow it to the town's ramp for vehicles. In many cases the mayor would loan a dump truck that for a smile would put the sand on church construction location. Then I would fly in with the portable block forms and sheet metal for the roof. We used all the free labor and Pentecostal zeal we could mix together to build.

Sometimes a church was built faster with boards taken from standing trees from nearby jungle. Environmental laws would not allow these trees to be cut down and exported, but law provisions allowed the locals to use lumber for their own buildings in the area without hassle. To feed the hardworking men, the local ladies made pots of rice and beans amidst the roar of power saws in the background. Many a time such a church was dedicated with a Cessna floatplane tied up in the current of the river in front.

Bennie's version of Instrument Flight Rules, or IFR, quickly became I Follow River. The seaplane and trained men rapidly helped to open churches in all directions from the home base in Manaus: in Autazes, Marrecão Island, Beiradão, Beruri, Canabuoca, Paratari, Maués, Maués-Mirim, Jacaré, Apoquitaua, Itacoatiara, Uricurituba, Urucará, Jeiteua, Caapiranga, Parintins, Eirunepé, Carauarí, Envira, Mourão, Santa Luzia, and other places. It was especially useful in transporting portable forms for making cement blocks.

They were "on duty" with the Cessna 172.

UPC of Brazil uses boats and seaplanes to serve 650 churches in the Amazon.

Building materials arrive for the new church in
Manaquiri.

Theresa receives used clothing to distribute in
Brazil.

Rescue on the Abonari River

When man tried to invade the vast Amazon rain forest with road equipment, it seemed all the elements fought back: impenetrable jungle, torrential rains, raging rivers, breath-sucking humidity, fierce Indians, snakes, jaguars, wild boars, alligators ... even mosquitos. Early in 1972, Bennie received a desperate phone call from Andre, an army officer in charge of a group of men building a temporary bridge over the Abonari River to the north of Manaus.

"Pastor Bennie, this is urgent!" the army official pleaded. "Fourteen men on my bridge-building crew have come down with malaria. The sick workers need medical supplies fast. The only solution to helping those men is to quickly get an aircraft that can land on water. Their radio went out days ago. Could you at least fly over their base camp and drop some supplies and check out the possibilities for airlifting the sick men out? From our last contact, we know that at least one has already died."

Bennie realized he would have to fly a single-engine seaplane for an hour and a half one-way over solid green jungle, his life hanging solely on the performance of a four-cylinder engine. The return without landing doubled the airtime to three hours. In that vast expanse, not even a faint sliver of open water existed on the horizon for an alternate "airport" for a seaplane.

Bennie tried to be polite in his refusal. "Our mission is basically of a religious nature. Can you remove your sick men by other means?" he asked.

"Considering the time element, no other means exist," the officer explained. "I tried to get a helicopter, but none is available. Ten sets of turbulent rapids block our access on the river. This would require loading and unloading the boat many times. The time, logistics, and work involved, as well as the possibility of mechanical failure or an accident en route, defy any other solution. On the return, it would be rough to operate a boat loaded with so many sick, helpless people with malaria, especially when those same sets of rapids would have to be portaged again."

This is one of those few times I wish I didn't have a mission floatplane, Bennie thought. *If only I were at a convention of our mission in Rio or São Paulo or on furlough! Most of the time the Cessna takes me safely where I point its nose, but this place is not one of them.*

"We are just a private, registered religious entity, and though I sympathize with the urgency of your needs, we could not fly for hire nor pay aircraft operational expenses on goodwill alone, even if it were possible for an aircraft to land on that narrow river," Bennie explained. "Even if all were favorable, the aircraft's capacity is too small. The pontoons add weight, increase air drag, and shorten the aircraft's range. That reduces the passenger capacity. I am sorry, but I can't help you."

Undaunted by Bennie's refusal, the officer showed up at the DeMerchants' home the next morning! He produced a copy from Aeronautics of an official telegram authorizing Bennie, if possible, to meet the needs of their present plight and any similar mercy missions.

"Pastor Bennie, we will supply the fuel for this operation. All we ask is that you fly an hour per barrel of fuel for us when we need your help. You can use the rest for your own mission."

Bennie felt his resistance slipping. That meant five hours of flying time for free! What a blessing in planting churches!

"Sir, that is very generous, but I have another problem," Bennie objected. "Customs has held up a new exhaust system for weeks because of some paperwork the mission does not have."

"We'll take care of that today," the officer said.

And they did.

Resigned, Bennie checked with his insurance, and they added coverage of the operation.

Bennie never saw government bureaucracy work so fast! In a short time he received delivery of seventeen barrels of aviation fuel. The army also placed fuel on a boat that would go all night at all speed to the nearest point to the Abonari River on the Apuau River lake that Bennie suggested might be a good location to air-jump the sick men in several trips from the bridge construction site.

The best practical route for building a road connecting Manaus to Boa Vista, capital of Roraima state, followed a terrain of high elevation through the jungle because farther west the Rio Negro's lowlands flooded in the rainy season. One major obstacle in sticking to this route through the jungle: the road would have to pass through the savage Atroari-Waimari Indian reserve.

These fierce, naked Indians, who lived two centuries or more in the past, could suddenly appear from upriver, paddling their long, straight dugout canoes without a whisper. They could put an arrow through the side of a rising fish when they waited less than thirty yards away with their arrows notched. They could meet the white man several times with a smile, swap gifts, and disappear into the jungle. No one could communicate with them. They only mimicked what was said, good or bad. Relations sizzled when they appeared with painted faces and bodies, and any suspicious move, when the Indians confirmed the civilized man was without a firearm nearby, could precipitate a rain of arrows.

Sixty miles south of where Bennie was to land on the Abonari, bulldozers and road equipment had reached the orange mud of hills in the jungle near Canoas Creek. The tops of these hills were deforested in a 230-foot-wide trans-Amazon highway right-of-way of huge, drying fallen trees. Road surveyors from the army had run the line and forged ahead with a special bridge-building crew walking several days to the Abonari River, where the highway would eventually cross.

About forty men had been working on the Abonari River bridge project, cutting selected termite-proof, hardwood lumber from the nearby jungle with chain saws. They hiked several days in the dry season, carrying food and supplies on the road survey line through the jungle. Now on location, isolated and working on the Abonari bridge project, the pay was good, but they felt their life was cheap.

From the Cessna floatplane, Bennie followed the swath through the jungle until it ended sixty miles south of the Abonari River. He breathed a sigh of relief when at last he spotted the silver thread of the river. He scrutinized the narrow river and glimpsed the work crew's shacks from the air. Hands with shirts or white towels waved from below!

Their excitement must not influence my decision, Bennie thought as he circled and studied the wind and the narrow river. *I am up here and I will decide whether it is go or no go!*

It was a tight place, but with maximum caution and at the slowest possible approach speed, Bennie felt it could be done. His main hang-up was that the place lacked a little bit of reserve space he always preferred to have that he calls "over-run." In this situation, he yearned for a longer bit of over-run!

Bennie stared at the landing point on the river and noted that a steady breeze was blowing riffles on the water. The smoke of a small cooking fire ascended in a slow, even slant in the jungle opening near the bridge site.

The shacks were located at a sharp turn at the upper end of this rare straight stretch of the narrow jungle river. The upper stretch was just long enough to land the seaplane using a low-speed, full-flap, power approach. Then, with the seaplane's speed reduced on the final part of the landing, Bennie must turn left and follow the narrow river's bed to a stop. At this stopping point, the river turned sharper to the right and narrowed further with high, overhanging trees. Their long, huge limbs reached across the river below them, as if they were trying to shake hands. At a glance Bennie further observed that this remaining space of such a "handshake" was less than the wingspan of the Cessna floatplane. If the landing did not go well, the luxury of coming up again for a better try had to be ruled out. There was a little over-run area before finally turning right at the end, but not much.

The Cessna 172's stall buzzer sounded like a doll-baby's cry as it came off and on in slow flight on the final flight leg of approach set up farther back than usual. Flaps were fully extended and the plane settled lower and lower with a nose-high attitude and the slight burr of a running engine. The headwind held moderate and steady. Trees passed slower below. As the last tree just above the shacks barely brushed behind the pontoons, Bennie thought out loud, "Don't freeze, work the rudders, keep it straight!"

The little plane sank beneath the hulking trees with their outstretched limbs. Its wings were level with the top of bushes close to the left. Nose up! Squash! On the water, the plane skied to a stop, shorter even than where Bennie had planned. The engine idled, cooling down, and the current of the rain-swollen river carried the plane downstream at a fast walking speed.

Bennie cut the engine and, as the propeller wound down, quickly grabbed the paddle. The river's current edged the seaplane's wing toward trees on the opposite bank. Bennie ran to the front of the pontoon, paddled the plane around, re-entered, re-started the engine, and taxied back against the current to the base camp.

When he climbed the riverbank, he found malaria-stricken men pallid with weakness, chills, or fever, lying with glazed eyes in hammocks in open-sided huts around the clearing. To them, the luxury of a hospital in Manaus seemed a dream.

Bennie discovered that the camp's SSB HF radio with wire antennas was strung from bushes outside. The battery at the base camp was discharged and their portable gasoline generator wouldn't work: this explained their inability to communicate with Manaus. Bennie unclipped the cover of the battery box, removed the floatplane's small aircraft battery from its metal box under the cowling, and carried it to their crude base camp of palm thatch. The radio came alive with the power from the battery. It whined and crackled with static as the base camp manager sounded off a few times in Portuguese.

"Manaus! Manaus! This is Abonari River calling!"

"Abonari, this is Manaus. You finally got on the air! Go ahead!"

"The seaplane just landed. At Abonari! He landed here on the river! We got everything you sent!"

The camp overseer was elated that Bennie got the little Cessna 172 into that tight location with some desperately needed emergency medical supplies. They had been waiting days without radio or personal contact.

The camp manager wanted to send all the sick out at once.

"I'll be glad to get any passenger out of this narrow river," Bennie cautioned him, "but not until I've inspected any obstacles I didn't see from the air, especially anything beneath the high trees on the lower far end of the landing area."

Taking a canoe, Bennie and the camp overseer paddled the entire length of the useful splashdown area and beyond. Bennie studied carefully from the canoe and mentally marked a leaning tree as the point the floatplane would come out from under the green canopy. This would be the go, no-go decision point. At this point Bennie had to be flying on takeoff each time to safely climb over obstacles ahead for clearance safety. If not flying at this point on take-off, he decided, he would cut power, stop on the remaining water space, lighten the plane's load, and try again.

His careful survey satisfied Bennie, and he warned the workers that their canoe must stay tied up at the river's bank till he was airborne.

"When I return for the next patients, I'll circle before landing to warn you that I'm coming in with pontoons that would be hard to rebuild if they hit your canoe," he cautioned them.

Threading this needle seven times, Bennie ferried the fourteen sick men, two at a time, from Abonari to the waiting boat on the Apuau River in one long, fast-moving, fifteen-hour day that started as the first weak glow of sunrise lightened the dark horizon and finished in the fading sunset. He rested only while the sick men were carried in hammocks to the plane's pontoon. At Apuau, where others from the large boat took the sick men aboard, Bennie refueled the plane, checked the oil, and inspected the fuel sumps for water.

The rest was routine: start up, taxi from the boat, turn into the wind, give a final check to the gauges, push full throttle again for takeoff. In the air, he established a second routine: a tuna sandwich when climb level was established, gulps of ice water from a four-liter thermos kept under the seat. At altitude, the air was cooler and he could relax, sit back, swish a handkerchief over a sweat-dripping face, and push up his moisture-flecked eyeglasses. He aimed the nose of the plane toward a distant jungle hill on the horizon that in half an hour of flying would be just to the right of the careful approach into Abonari River.

Between two of these forty-five-minute trips ferrying the sick men, Bennie was standing on the left pontoon of the plane when an astonished Brazilian putt-putted his heavily-laden aluminum canoe onto the river bank. Bennie smiled to himself at the man's incredulous gaze.

"Who are you? Did you fly that plane here? How did you manage to land on this narrow river?" The questions tumbled from this short, strong man with thinning dark hair.

Bennie introduced himself and answered the man's questions. He learned he was talking to Gilberto, who worked with the National Indian Foundation (FUNAI).

"My job is to pacify the Indians before the jungle crews of surveyors, right-of-way cutters, and road crews with the bulldozers, earth-movers, earth packers, and such arrive in their reserve," Gilberto explained. "I hope to get them to agree for the road to pass through their area."

Gilberto planned every move in friendly contacts with the Indians. He hoped to use his friendship to try to settle the Indians into smaller manageable groups and provide some of their basic food and health needs. The direct contact of these Indians with hundreds of workers along the road could be devastating to the project with the outcome of inexperienced workers mixing with some of these almost naked Indian women and children.

"My men and I came here by river in the heat, portaging ten sets of rapids. It has taken us more than a week of backbreaking work," Gilberto related. "You say this place is only an hour and a half from Manaus by plane? Man, I need your help!"

Bennie mulled that one over as he finished evacuating the malaria-stricken men. Would this be another opportunity to win souls? Could these savage Indians Gilberto told him about be reached with the gospel?

The colonel in charge of the Abonari River operation was pleased that Bennie got all the sick men out of the camp in one day. Later, Bennie received a document from the army, renewed annually and authorizing him to leave the mission aircraft anytime at their transport division's headquarters, where many a night an armed soldier standing nearby guarded it while Bennie slept soundly and peacefully at home.

2008 update: Today, BR-174 stretches from Manaus to Boa Vista, capital of the state of Roraima, Brazil's northernmost state that borders Venezuela. Even with the asphalt road, all general, public-use traffic is closed through the Indian reserve between sunset and sunrise.

Bennie air-dropped medicines to wild Amazon tribes.

DeMerchant family visits the
Hiscariaros on Nhamunda River

Piranha church on Eiru River near Eirunepé

11

Wild Indians

Bennie, seeing Gilberto's dire need for a floatplane for his work, was glad to use his flying skills to aid his friend. Winning souls was Bennie's mission, and Indians have souls, Bennie reasoned. Any point of goodwill Gilberto won with them would transfer to Bennie as well.

In his method of trying to pacify the Atroaris and Waimiris along the northern rivers, Gilberto would fly over with Bennie, with the plane loaded with presents. These could be machetes, axes, fishing lines, hooks, and other small items like sugar or candy or things that would not break with the airdrop. The Indians loved mirror-like objects to see their faces, and flat files with which to sharpen knives. Bennie would circle the *malocas*, the huge, round, thatch-roofed huts where their families lived inside in pie-slice-shaped sectors. If it were the first flyover, the Indians, on hearing the sound of the plane, would flock outside and nervously run around or down the short wider trails into the nearby jungle. As a precaution, some of the men picked up their bows and arrows. On three occasions when Bennie came in too quickly, an Indian in the shaded eave of the overhanging thatch pulled the bow back and let fly a warning arrow toward the plane. It was fascinating to see the small arrow grow bigger as it neared the flying airplane, stall, and slide toward the ground fifty yards below.

The naked, brawny, brown bodies of the men could be seen from the air in a low pass, sometimes with their leader standing on a high stump, waving his arms. Some held up stalks of green bananas or Brazil nuts in their heavy round casings that held them inside like the sections of an orange. Others would hold up thin white manioc cakes that looked like hardened pancakes.

"That is their way of saying they want to trade their items with mine," Gilberto explained. After emptying the contents of the plane a safe distance into their jungle clearing, he would ask Bennie to take him back to the river nearby, where he had his boat and crew. Then, with his crew, Gilberto would go as close as possible by water, and the men would start their trek through the jungle for final contact and friendship with these indigenous people on the ground. Dropping presents from the air before going into these places on foot seemed to send a friendly message, but no one really knew what the savage Indians were thinking.

The Indians used the river as their highway. They could suddenly appear at a new hunting or fishing spot in their *ubas,* or long, dugout canoes. From the air the ubas looked like matchsticks. The sides were rounded like a tree trunk. The bottom, thicker and heavier than the sides, made the canoe difficult to upset. Ten men could squat on its floor, one behind the other, and rapidly paddle with their families and belongings from one hunting area to another.

At the Abonari bridge site, men guarded the trail entrances to the camp and the bridge as well. On one overnight trip to the Abonari bridge site, while walking around in the early evening darkness before going to his hammock, Bennie chatted with these uniformed armed guards.

"Why should anyone be afraid of Indians when firearms are on hand for protection?" he asked.

"An Indian can sneak along barefoot through the jungle, feeling his every step," the guard replied. "He has lived his life there and knows how to hunt and survive from or even kill jaguars with bows and arrows. He avoids stepping on twigs or brushing against branches, knows when to run quickly or not move for hours. He can be camouflaged and never make a sound. He can hide behind foliage in the jungle shade with his eye watching your every move through a slot of light. He can have a bow drawn with an arrow's shank resting on his thumb. When he is sure that the second is right, he can silently shoot, and though a guard have a machine gun, he will only feel the arrow pierce when it is too late. When a firearm goes off, everyone is awakened to this signal of danger in the area. But these silent figures with a history of massacres can cause trouble!"

When Sister Margaret heard about the Abonari bridge site, she wanted to see this place. So one day Bennie took off with Theresa, Sister Margaret, and young daughters Beth and Pam for a two-hour spin over the green jungle to land on the Alalau and to be with a small group of these Atroaris-Waimiris Indians who came for food and other items at the right-of-way camp. They wandered peaceably in and out of the camp. Rumors maintained that these Indians were afraid they would lose their wives to the white man's invasion with jungle cutters and road workers. Bennie wanted to dispel that idea by showing off his wife and family. After being with the Indians a few hours without incident, the DeMerchant group flew back to Manaus before sunset.

While stopped one time on the Alalau River to pick up fuel that he had hidden in the jungle in plastic jerry jugs to increase the floatplane's range for a trip, Bennie thought he heard birds chattering around the river's bend. While Bennie was pouring fuel through the wing's chamois, about ten Indians appeared in a dugout canoe from upriver. Before landing, Bennie had circled and had not seen a canoe in the area. He didn't care to have any unnecessary contacts with them alone, especially on that day because Raimundo, the teenage son of the man who took care of Bennie's plane, had begged to accompany Bennie. But Bennie knew that when the Indians heard the rumble of a distant aircraft, they could quickly paddle from the middle of the river and hide themselves under the overhanging jungle foliage at the narrow river's edge.

As they appeared, Bennie yanked the funnel out of the wing tank, tossed the empty six-gallon containers into the plane, and tried to act nonchalant. The turn was just ahead and the Indians were paddling fast in his direction. It was too late to make a quick takeoff upriver because the Indians were in the middle of the "runway," and rocks and rapids scoured the water below. They approached the plane's pontoon on the right, striking hard enough with the canoe's bow to dent it lightly. Two of the men jumped on the pontoon while another wrapped a tough vine around the float's front aluminum rope cleat. The plane's light anchor strained with the added weight of their canoe in the river's current. They had apparently come from working above at their small jungle clearing and had green and ripe bananas, long root potatoes, some land turtles, a small alligator, and a few dead wild pigs shaded under some leaves. Their bows and arrows lay in the bottom of the boat.

They were on the pilot's side and Bennie sat facing them through the open door. They appeared excited and wanted to trade something. One held up a stalk of green bananas as two others curiously stared at objects inside the plane's open door and the round glass dials of the aircraft's instrument panel. Bennie finally eased out of his seat while they stepped back on the pontoon. Accepting their stalk of bananas, he placed it on the floor behind his seat. While bent over, he found in the seat's back pocket all the Nestle chocolate bars that he carried for survival in case he had to miss a meal while flying.

Grabbing the candy bars, he stepped out, distributed them, pulled up the anchor, and untied their vine rope.

When he opened the door to return, two or three more Indians jumped back on the pontoon and held the canoe alongside with their feet. Then another jumped on, and the top of the pontoon sank almost level with the water-line. The wing tip on Bennie's side dipped toward the water with their added weight while the other wing slanted upward, toward the trees. Through the door's open window, Bennie glanced forward and saw no one standing near the propeller's arc. He pulled on the master switch and turned the key to start!

The solenoid gave off its unusual "tunng," and the propeller slowly spun with the mixture rich and the throttle control advanced. In about three turns of the propeller, white smoke billowed from the exhaust as the engine fired. The Indians on the pontoon jumped into their dugout as the plane surged upward and rocked in the water. By some chance the plane's nose was still headed upriver at a manageable maneuvering angle for the water rudders to turn the wings away from the overhanging branches, and the floatplane's tail cleared the Indians' heavy canoe.

Bennie dropped the flaps and hit full takeoff power at the same time with one hand! As the plane cleared the trees in takeoff from this infamous Alalau River, Bennie glanced at his speechless passenger. Raimundo was as white as a manioc cake!

Gilberto thought that seeing the whole DeMerchant family would have a positive effect on some of these Indians, so he asked Bennie to fly

Maroaga and Comprido, the heads of the tribe, to Manaus to see civilization for the first time. They had never ridden in a plane, and Bennie had quite an experience with them. They cringed when he gave the plane engine full throttle and they started speeding down the narrow Alalau River and soared into the air. Bennie knew how they must have felt to see the ground drop below and the plane bank in a turn toward the south. Naturally, they leaned for the higher side. But after some time they seemed to realize that no harm was going to come to them.

The plan included flying almost two hours toward Manaus over the seventy-meter-wide jungle road right-of-way to the point where bulldozers were opening the road and farther to where vehicles were operating. Thus, these Indians would see the "big trail" through their jungle. They observed the cars and trucks that the white man used to transport his things and by seeing this they might understand that a big trail was now being built between Manaus and Boa Vista 450 miles to the north on the other side of the equator.

Bennie landed with the two Indian chiefs in Manaus. They seemed to have survived the trip. However, they were now in the outskirts of the city and would be riding from the floating hangar to the offices of FUNAI. Except for their permanent vine around their waist they were naked. Bennie found some work trousers in the hangar and somehow persuaded them to put these on over their thick vine belts. They climbed the hill on foot to his waiting pick-up truck. Bennie opened the door on their side since they didn't even know what to touch. He patted the seat for them to get in and sit while he walked around to his door on the opposite side. When he opened the door they were squatting on the seat with their feet under them. So when Bennie got in he placed his feet on the floor, and they understood the modern, civilized way of sitting.

When the pickup motor started, the chiefs looked uneasy, but as the truck inched along this back road toward the city, they began taking it all in stride. Bennie came to the stop sign and then entered the asphalted two-way road. As a car neared them from the opposite direction his passengers cringed and edged away from Bennie, but the car passed them and the Indians relaxed. Halfway to the city Bennie stopped at a small stand and bought three cold Cokes and opened them, sticking straws into each bottle. As he sipped the liquid, the Indians imitated him. However, the carbonated beverage fizzed out of their noses.

When Bennie stopped at a traffic light, he pointed out that it was red and the other cars crossed the intersection while he waited. When it turned green, the car ahead did not move. Bennie tapped the horn, and the Indian beside him, mimicking Bennie's action, put his hand on the horn and laughed for a long time while it honked. The stalled car's chauffer looked around and scowled.

At home, after the chiefs eyed Bennie's big German shepherd dog as he sniffed them, Bennie turned Maroaga and Comprido over to the National Indian Foundation personnel, who took them to the Indian department and half-way house where they ate and spent the night in hammocks. The next day they got a grand tour of Manaus and visited several stores. A day later the foundation phoned Bennie.

"Fly these Indians back to the jungle. They wanted to carry everything out of the stores they entered. These Indians are running across the streets in the middle of downtown like rabbits, dodging in and around moving cars, trucks, and buses. If a car injures one or both of them, the result of the trip will be counterproductive to our plans," they explained.

Their trip back to the jungle was uneventful other than as soon as they saw their people they quickly peeled off their trousers and reverted to their same skimpy native attire. But even that familiarization with civilization trip didn't deter the Indians from their massacring ways.

2008 updates: The Indians eventually did stop their massacres. Several of the native children are named Bennie. DeMerchant's greatest hope is that they will be named of Jesus in the waters of baptism and receive the Holy Spirit.

At this time the mission working with Brazilians has about one thousand Indians of other tribal areas in Amazonas state near Maués and on the upper Solimões and Juruá Rivers. Another group that was removed from the upper Rio Negro settled near Manaus, and several, through contacts with one of our Manaus pastors, have come to God. Three have graduated from the ABI two-year course in Manaus and want to reach more of their own people; in 2008, they started their own Bible school near Manaus with twenty-four first-year students.

Time for coffee at UPC Matamatá Madeira River

Brother Jurandir works with a thousand Indians.

A
Harrowing Story

Bennie and his family were seated around the lunch table when they heard someone clapping his hands at the driveway's iron gate. The callers were Gilberto and Andre.

"Gilberto, come sit and have lunch with us!" Bennie invited his visitors. "We'll put more water in the soup!"

"No, Pastor Benee," Gilberto replied. "I already ate. Go ahead and we'll wait here on the sofa, but we need you urgently! We have a report of a problem at the Alalau outpost. We must check it out."

As Bennie quickly finished his lunch, he recalled a trip into Indian territory he had made just a month earlier. Bennie had flown Gilberto to the outpost on the Alalau River on January 7. They arrived late in the afternoon with some needed supplies from the city. Gilberto worked most of the evening and talked a lot with the four groups that manned the outpost, while Bennie sat in a hammock and tried to smile and communicate with six Indians who had floated from upriver in their dugout canoes and planned to leave in the morning. Finally the Indians went to their lean-to in the small clearing and slept in their coarse vine hammocks while Bennie went to sleep.

But it could cost dearly to wrongly guess the motivations of wild Indians! They were treacherous people. From his own experience, Bennie knew they could smile and shake hands, but in less than an hour any suspicious move on the visitor's part could cause hidden bows and arrows to appear from behind fallen logs or jungle foliage.

As soon as the three men were airborne, Gilberto revealed the harrowing adventure of one of his crew members at the Alalau outpost. The treacherous Atroari Indians returned on January 17 without their women and children, and that alone should have signaled that something was not as before.

The outpost workers were working nearby on the camp's duties outside. While the Indians mingled with the FUNAI workers and diverted their attention, one Indian slipped into the house and hid the firearms. After making signs that they were leaving on a hunting trip, the Indians all began to melt back into the jungle. Then, suddenly, they reappeared with bows and arrows and attacked. Two of the men of Gilberto's team died near the river. Another died instantly just a few feet from the door of the outpost while running to it for safety.

The fourth man, Louis, fled to the outpost, flung himself inside and slammed the door shut. He knew all of his friends had been killed. Through the cracks of the boards of the house, he heard their screams and saw the Indians dancing on his friends' arrow-bristled bodies as they died.

Louis searched inside frantically for a weapon and found none. He could see through the cracks as the Indians danced for joy on his companions. The thatched roof of the outpost burst into flames from a burning torch. Louis found some firecrackers, hurriedly lit them, slid the wooden window back, and hurled them out the window at the attackers. The firecrackers exploded in a string, all at once, while the Indians quickly retreated toward the jungle.

His chance for escape now or never, Louis groped through the smoke of the burning house and reached the door facing the river. He dashed to the bank and flung himself into the water. A strong swimmer, he swam underwater until he was well over halfway across as the current carried him down the stream. When he surfaced for a gulp of air, an Indian spotted him and called the other Indians to the chase.

When Louis dived under again he saw several arrows hit the water where he had been. Some Indians raced to the end of the short clearing downriver from the burning house, and as Louis reached the opposite bank he saw several of them untying the aluminum canoe. Fortunately for him, as they all jumped in it on one side, it upset and dumped them into the water. Used to their dugout ubas cut from tree trunks, with thick stabilizing bottoms, they didn't expect the white man's aluminum canoe to tip them into the river.

Louis clambered from the river and plunged into the jungle farther below and on the opposite side. Taking the sun for a general direction, he ran as fast and as far as he could to put distance between himself and the murdering Indians. When he felt he was well covered with the jungle, he hid deep in the bush and never moved till midnight.

Louis reached the road right-of-way further south and eventually got to Manaus seventeen days later and told the FUNAI officials his incredible story.

"The FUNAI officials want to verify Louis's story," Gilberto explained as the plane sliced through the air above the jungle. "There has been no radio contact with the outpost from FUNAI's office in Manaus since that day, but it is not uncommon for a radio component to be defective, a battery to run down, or a generator problem to appear. We go to investigate."

Gilberto didn't speak much during the nearly two-hour trip over the jungle that afternoon to the Alalau River. Bennie sensed that when Gilberto was quiet, he was tired, making plans, or nervous since he usually asked Bennie a lot of questions about flying time and distances to places in the Indian reserve.

As the small clearing near the highway bridge site on the Alalau rose over the nose of the plane, Bennie saw Gilberto reach behind and pull out two holsters with a loaded revolver in each. As Gilberto pulled his belt off and threaded its ends through each holster and rebuckled the belt, Bennie began to wonder. The head of the Abonari outpost, in the rear seat, already had his guns in place and was searching in the baggage area behind his seat for a shotgun. Sensing the tension, Bennie queried, with a smile, "O que voces vao fazer ... sequestrar o aviao?" which translates to, "What are you fellows going to do ... highjack the plane?"

Bennie circled the plane with the clearing on Gilberto's side so he could see better, and he finally broke his silence. "No, Benee, this is serious business. We have to carefully check out the report of this massacre."

Bennie circled the clearing several more times with the Cessna floatplane while the three men stared at the ashes of what had been the outpost building. It had burned flat. They searched the area and the horizon for a sign of smoke. There was none. There were no canoes in the river, and nothing moved in the empty clearing below.

After landing in the pond area of the river just below the location of the burned-out outpost, Bennie thought, *What if we need to get away in a hurry?* This river that could be a raging current with water above its banks was now low, with steep, high banks. Big boulders at a turn in the river just above the outpost blocked a quick takeoff in that direction, and the wind blew the wrong way for making a fast takeoff down the river to the boulders at the end of the pond below.

In front of the site, the huge trunk of a fallen tree whose upper end was underwater bridged the bank at a shallower incline than the steep bank itself. It served as the spot to tie up the plane on arrival and a natural ramp to walk up to the clearing above. The two men climbed out and slowly approached the top, walking on the angled tree trunk while Bennie tied up the plane. When they reached the top of the bank and walked through the small clearing, their heads disappeared. Then Bennie followed them. They walked to the charred remains of the outpost where Bennie had spent the night on the previous trip. It was nothing but ashes. The men noticed other areas where fires had burned.

Bennie looked down at the skull and vertebrae of the body of Ernesto left in the ashes, but the ribs and parts of his arms and legs were gone. He had fallen about three yards from where Bennie had hung his hammock and slept with the man's murderers nearby.

Gilberto took pictures of everything, but they touched nothing.

The Atroaris Indians had made many massacres in this region since 1911, four of which had occurred in 1973, and Bennie had just seen the evidence of the latest one.

When Bennie lay to sleep in his own bed that night, remembering what he had seen during the day, he pinched himself hard on the wrist and asked himself, "Was today really February 3, 1973?" He found it difficult to fall asleep because, when he closed his eyes, the revolting scenes at the outpost kept scrolling through his mind.

Will we ever be able to reach such treacherous, murderous people with the saving, life-changing gospel of Jesus Christ? he wondered.

Oswaldina and the Stolen Aviation Fuel

The story of God's church will be one of ongoing conflict, fierce battles, and agonizing tests of faith before its eventual victory. God could blast Satan away, and we could all smile, cross our arms, and walk into His immense wealth to a warless victory. But the story grows more glorious if He chooses to use one of His weakest things to confound the wise and glorify Himself (I Corinthians 1:27). The DeMerchants' struggle to plant and to husband an indigenous church in the rivers of Brazil's western Amazon verifies that principle.

Ilha de Marrecão Island, "the island of the black wild duck," was built by shifting river currents that deposited silt from the changing Solimões River sixty miles west of Manaus. Water covers it in the rainy season, so the inhabitants build their homes on stilts three to six feet above the ground. In the swollen river, anacondas and other snakes wash down to lodge under these houses. There they often rest in the day's warm temperature, out of sight. Edging up under the two-by-fours or some beam, the serpents will silently wait in the darkness for their small prey to appear from the river's floating grass. Bennie heard stories of mothers who left their babies asleep in a hammock only to find later the hammock empty and the babies nowhere to be found.

Some of the people left the island to live with relatives on higher ground for a few weeks until the water receded enough that they could plant their main cash crop of jute. At the jute harvest, after a grueling year of poverty, all had money for a few days to pay off the creditors who had trusted these hardworking people for months. So they floated downriver to pay their bills and to buy supplies.

The DeMerchants' work in this island was initiated by a family from Manacapuru, who went there in small canoes, paddling sometimes ten miles or more against the currents in the heat of the afternoon. Zeal kept them going. They wanted to hold house meetings in the homes of these island folk who, while in Manacapuru to purchase supplies, mingled in the crowds at street meetings as Bennie preached and Theresa pumped an accordion and sang. From such sometimes seemingly futile street meetings in town, visitors from the island invited church members to come to have meetings in their stilt houses.

Amidst small talk, the families socialized by drinking coffee and sharing the bread they had bought hot at the bakery in a plastic bag and a few kilograms of margarine in wax paper. They started by singing choruses and after a while testified of their experiences with God, how they found Him and prayed, and that He filled them with the Holy Ghost. They would always read a psalm or some other uplifting passage of Scripture and add their comments. It wasn't preaching, but it was getting there!

After a number of meetings of this sort, their pastor, Brother Manuel, would come from Manacapuru by small, powered canoes and join the fellowship. Then Bennie's Cessna seaplane would anchor in the backwaters near the floating grass, and a missionary with workers would follow up on this constantly growing number of people, many of whom had already received their personal Pentecost.

These people, who struggled to survive on their ever-changing, nine-mile-long island of silt, loved prayer meetings. Their fervent prayers plowed the fertile ground for revival farther west in the Amazon. For God to choose such dwellers of the Amazon's lowlands that silt changed annually and who had nothing "fixed" in this life was only His divine work. They prayed many a night in long, hard intercessory prayer meetings that could be heard from their open windows far across the waters to the "mainland" of the river. Soaked in sweat from head to foot, they prayed. Their voices became hoarse from crying out to God.

After building a long wooden church to accommodate their growing numbers there, the DeMerchants also built a small wooden parsonage—on stilts, of course! Bennie purchased a kerosene refrigerator and gas stove that their church boat delivered. The men of the church painted and fixed up the building with hammock hooks for Sister Margaret, who would be flown to Marrecão with a helper, baggage, food, and hammocks. Sister Margaret and her helper would spend a week at a time in children's meetings before Bennie returned to minister and fly them back to her apartment above their home in Manaus.

Sister Margaret held her listeners spellbound as she told exciting Bible stories and illustrated the story on the flannelboard. Her audience grew daily as the women and men sidled in, sat in the back seats, and then moved forward when others standing on the steps outside could not get in but just "wanted to see."

"Brother Bennie, I'm embarrassed to teach the children simple Bible truths and see the building filling with adults who came in the daytime heat! Such a meeting in America for adults would almost be a waste of time," Sister Margaret admitted.

However, the people hungered for more teaching of the Word to mix with their zealous prayer, so Bennie was invited to a New Year's church meeting on Marrecão Island in 1973. During the service, some of the believers were given an opportunity to testify. As they did so, Bennie noticed a common thread in their themes. Most of them had come from the upper Juruá River and its tributaries. They testified of having received the great salvation of the Holy Ghost on this island, but they lamented the relatives they left in Eirunepé and the other rural areas around this city of ten degrees longitude farther west from Manaus.

Bennie listened. *These testimonies were almost all the same,* he thought. *They all want to know who will go back to tell their relatives about what they have received.*

Their testimonies jolted Bennie into a new pattern of thinking. *I am a missionary. I have support. I have an airplane. Going to the upper Juruá River is a long distance to fly in a slow floatplane, but if we are to work in the Amazon in these far-out places, there has to be a starting point. Someone of courage will have to break the ice and go there.*

So after hearing these testimonies of missionary burden, Bennie decided to involve them in helping support a missionary, one of their own in this far-off city of Eirunepé in the middle of the "big rubber" country. He presented them with a plan.

"If you will supply funds to help support two young men who are soon coming out of Bible school, I will fly them to Eirunepé and visit them occasionally," he promised.

After that promise to them in the meeting in the island church, Bennie began to think it through. In Manaus, he laid World Aeronautical Charts for the region on his table. The huge maps curled over the table halfway to the floor. A trip to Eirunepé was no flying around a local airport or barnyard, but a flight that jets would normally take. It would be a tedious flight for a slow-flying Cessna 172. Obtaining fuel would be a problem on a river where a barge took nearly six weeks to navigate the same distance.

To safely fly this trip with a minimum of the "Green Hell" going beneath the Cessna floatplane's wings required a nine-hour flight trip one way. Even then, following the rivers to jump over points left more of the green floor to fly over than Bennie preferred. Flying in the height of the rainy season when 120 or more inches of rain fell in about six months could mean possibly flying all day in the rain. To not visually lose the river in the rains meant flying low. At such times, looking out the side windows offered a better view. The greatest advice of one visual pilot to another was "Keep the tank full and do not lose the river."

"I mused afterward, as I studied charts and considered that no commercial airlines flew at the time to that place, that, given the problem of fuel availability, maybe I had bitten off more than I could chew," DeMerchant admits.

However, he arranged for fuel to be transported by barges and stored on Marrecão Island. The church there helped with their support for the two workers. For a while the new work in Eirunepé went well and a wooden building the workers bought with some help from the DeMerchants' international friends and relatives filled up. Bennie would visit occasionally and enjoy preaching to the people. The work spread to rural areas near the city.

The workers in this far-removed place labored hard with generally poor results. An overdose of festive nightlife seemed to permeate the entire city, and it was difficult for the gospel to work with the constant shift in population. At times the work was left for months with no pastor. Some of the property they bought was taken over by invaders as construction for a new airport tore up the street.

Bennie made frequent runs to Eirunepé in the seaplane and stopped at other new works on the way, sometimes flying thirty-five hours to make a round-trip, flying by day, fueling up and preaching at night. Flight hours accumulated fast, and in four years he flew almost three thousand hours. He ferried fuel by barges to many distant towns along the Amazon, where he always stored a few barrels in a shed behind the church and under a canvas where he gassed up at night by jerry jugs and siphon hose to be ready to go at the first crack of dawn to the next church.

One of the few ladies in this pastorless church was Sister Oswaldina. This hardworking, courageous mother and grandmother received the Holy Ghost in her jungle home near the city.

"It seemed like the end of the world when I arrived in my Cessna floatplane and ministered," Bennie recalls. "With the workers gone, it seemed that small work had no future without a trained worker to remain. In such remote places with no fellowship, church leaders have to be men of will and be strong in the faith and for God. Then from the congregation came this one little woman—Oswaldina!"

The baptism of the Holy Ghost changed her life, and she bubbled with enthusiasm. More than a year went by, and her husband was still unsaved. Her older daughters were not interested in following a new faith, especially with so few people and no leader, choosing rather those carnival festivities and weekend dances at the nearby village. The local priest heard what had happened to Oswaldina and warned her of what could happen when she left their church and joined those Protestants, who had come like invaders from the outside world.

Sister Oswaldina traveled on the river in a small boat propelled by a shaft-driven inboard diesel marine engine. One day she bent to pick up something her smaller children had dropped on the floor of the boat. The turning shaft caught her long hair and abruptly scalped her, leaving only the shining bone of her head from over her eyebrows to the nape of her neck. A long trip to the hospital brought her little help. The doctors tried to graft skin to this open area, but it never really healed. From then on she always wore a towel wrapped around her head to protect the top of her head from the hot tropical sun, flies in the daytime, and mosquitoes at night.

Undeterred, Sister Oswaldina, always smiling and happy, would carry an umbrella in one hand and would trudge over a mile in rain, wading through mud holes while shepherding her small children along the town's torn-up streets that rain left impassible for vehicles. But she wanted to be on time for prayer service.

After flying solo in his Cessna 172 seaplane through an electrical storm so turbulent that he turned back for a while, Bennie became very discouraged with the complications from the work. The matter was compounded when he realized that someone had trespassed onto their lot and erected a new fence before the lot was properly registered. Contesting this trespass would be next to impossible, but the trespass cut drastically into the area needed for the building. To deepen his depression, Bennie discovered someone else had stolen the only four remaining barrels of aviation fuel sent by barge weeks earlier that would have fueled his return to Manaus.

Bennie mixed auto fuel with his remaining fuel to get over the long trek of jungle and river back to the next refueling point. He stood on the wing strut of the floatplane, watching the last of the fuel trickle through the chamois on the funnel and into the wing tank and thought, *No worker to continue. I cannot take any more of this. I will not come back to this distant, expensive town.*

But how would he face Oswaldina and tell her that? He had pondered this while trying to go to sleep in the hammock in a neighboring house that night across the river from her humble jungle cottage.

As the fog wisps were lifting from the river and the sun rising higher, Bennie heard a beautiful church hymn. Sister Oswaldina, with a towel wrapped around her head, trilled a song of praise as she hand washed her clothes in the brown water of the Juruá River from a small wooden dock.

"We will pray for you to have a safe trip back to Manaus and that you will get fuel and can still visit us and preach," she exclaimed after Bennie told her he was giving up on the church there and, due to the stolen fuel, would not return. That small woman with all kinds of problems in life watched as he pushed the plane's pontoons from the shore and said goodbye for what he expected would be a long time.

He climbed to a safe height before leaving the security of the river beneath and took a direct compass course to the next stop. As the sun rose higher, the jungle beneath him burst into every shade of green, and he felt a bit secure with cooler air. At least, he would have a few minutes to pray if the engine quit!

Bennie began to think about all that had happened. Here he was, a big, healthy, strong North American ... and Oswaldina, frail, sick, but working diligently and still singing. Hours before he arrived, an anaconda had slithered out of the river and coiled around one of her chickens. Quickly she grabbed the old, rusty, three-piece shotgun at the back of the house and at close range killed the snake and released the chicken. Though alone all day, and sometimes alone all night and with three small grandchildren to protect, she would not surrender her possessions without a fight. Sister Oswaldina didn't know the word "quit."

After Bennie returned from the nine-hour flight, he was tired of flying and decided to work on the construction of a large church in Manaus in a new suburb of the city. A couple of weeks later while he was laying cement blocks, a Volkswagon Bug taxi drove up with a good-sized passenger, who exited the taxi, straightened, and strode over to observe Bennie, who, with trowel in hand, was trying to lay cement blocks along the stretched line.

"Are you Bennie? Bennie the missionary? Bennie the pilot?" The urgency in his voice was unmistakable.

"Well, right now, I am Bennie the bricklayer!" Bennie replied and quickly added that he had just returned from a ver-r-r-y long flying trip.

The man represented a global insurance company that had underwritten the hull insurance of a Grecian-registered ship. Several days before, it had loaded thousands of tons of Peruvian plywood 1,200 miles above Manaus at Iquitos, Peru. The captain had tried navigating the Amazon River at night.

"The crew was drinking, and about five hundred miles west of Manaus, they steered the ship out of the main channel of the river in the night and ran aground in the shoals," the insurance adjuster explained.

Stuck in the mud with the current pushing the boat forward from behind, the propellers of the craft did not have enough traction to pull the ship backward. To complicate matters, the Amazon was dropping several inches a day and the ship was stuck in the mud of the river's bottom in only about eighteen to twenty feet of water. This insurance investigator had flown four thousand miles extra on commercial airlines to arrive in Manaus a few hours earlier than the scheduled direct flight in order to probe any damage to this ship's hold.

Bennie had been flying and gone so often, solving church problems or making free humanitarian flights to help victims of accident, injury, disease, or death, that he frequently felt guilty of neglect when he left his two daughters for days at a time when they needed a daddy at home.

"I wanted to say, 'No, get a fast speedboat and let me work here in the city on my church construction,'" Bennie recalls.

The adjuster, however, waved a heavy bit of leverage in front of Bennie. "You are playing here with peanuts laying these blocks while we have the risk of millions of dollars of loss! Come and put me on this ship we underwrote that is stuck in the mud or whatever, and we will help you on your church work!"

The full moon brightened the Amazon as the Cessna purred for hours 'til what looked like a lighted village blazed in the middle of the river. Yes, it was the sought-for ship! Bennie eased toward the water shining in the moonlight. Then he taxied upriver against the current toward the mass of the ship. A small boat motored to meet them. After mooring the plane with an anchor, Bennie clambered aboard the small craft that carried them to a hanging rope ladder. Swinging in the moonlight, Bennie climbed the ladder, not daring to look down until he reached the deck of the ship above, where he was ushered into first-class captain's quarters, ate a good meal, and slept the balance of the night.

During the night, the insurance investigator examined the ship from within its holds and returned hours later, relieved that up to then no damage had been done to the hull of the ship. But it would need powerful tugboats to move the ship and its load off the muddy bottom of the Amazon.

For the possibility of necessary future trips in the floatplane, the investigator ordered fuel for 150 hours of flying. This was unloaded into one of Bennie's pastor's boats to be sent upriver at all speed because of the oncoming dry season and lowering of the river. Later the rains came, and the ship floated free. The company donated all the barrels of fuel located at several points upstream—toward Eirunepé.

Bennie took years to burn all that fuel servicing the work in Eirunepé, Oswaldina's town, the town of the stolen aviation fuel.

Before Sister Oswaldina went to be with the Lord, Bennie told her how her prayers solved the fuel problem and moved the hand of God.

"She asked me to pray for her family members who had not yet received the great Pentecostal experience," Bennie remembers.

Years later and hundreds of miles downriver, in Coari, a city where revival has come and twelve churches dot the city alone, a well-dressed woman walked up to Bennie after he preached and shook his hand.

"I am Oswaldina's daughter," she said. "God found me, and my husband and I are in the church here in Coari!"

Oswaldina. Who could forget the frail, little grandmother, her scalped head wrapped in a towel, who slogged through the mud with three small grandchildren in tow because she refused to be late to a prayer meeting?

Oswaldina. See what her prayers had wrought!

2008 update: Today there are twenty-five churches and three Bible schools in the Juruá River area.

Water taxis in Amazon towns

Pioneer pastor Rafael opened several
works in Ceará state.

"My Lord Knows the Way through the Wilderness"

Theresa is Bennie's first line of defense. Rock steady and upbeat, she shoulders his responsibilities when mission work calls him aloft. One morning in November 1973, as she was cleaning the bedroom, a thought intruded into her mind: *You will bury your mother.*

She stopped, dustcloth poised over the dresser. *How can that be?* she wondered. *I don't know if my mom is even sick!*

A few weeks later while she was driving to the post office with four-year-old Pam, she started to sing, "My Lord knows the way through the wilderness; all I have to do is follow."

Well, for goodness sake! she thought. *Where did that song come from? I haven't sung that in years!*

But as soon as she opened the post office box and picked up the telegram from her sister, she realized that through that song the Lord was leading her.

"Mom passed away after surgery. Please come." The telegram was two days old.

Theresa spotted a friend in the post office. "Is there a flight to Miami today?" she asked.

"There's one at noon," he answered.

Theresa glanced at the clock. It was already 10 AM. She raced home, grabbed her passport, and floorboarded the car to the police station, where she filled out a migratory tax form to pay in cash at the bank for an exit stamp on her passport later at the airport. By stating that she had an emergency, she was able to get in front of a long line at the bank to pay this tax. Then she rushed back home to pack a suitcase for cold weather for her and Beth. She arranged for Pam to stay with her housekeeper. Bennie was out of town, and she had no way to contact him. She tried to call her family, but her mother had moved from Wisconsin, and Theresa's brothers had gone to get her body.

Fortunately, Bennie arrived in time to race her to the airport. But at the ticket counter, she met another obstacle.

"I'm sorry, ma'am," the ticket agent told her, "but there are no available seats on the plane."

Yet the song persisted: *My Lord knows the way through the wilderness; all I have to do is follow... .*

Then a reprieve came! The plane was delayed until midnight.

"Go to the agency, and buy your ticket," the agent advised Theresa. "Someone will probably cancel his reservation because of the delay." So Theresa hurried to buy two tickets.

Another reprieve! A friend asked the pastor to delay the funeral until the afternoon of Theresa's arrival in Madison, Wisconsin. And Theresa's friends at ABI helped fund her airfare and buy winter clothes for her and Beth.

Yet the song persisted: *My Lord knows the way through the wilderness; all I have to do is follow... .*

"My dad had passed away four years earlier while I was in Brazil and I could not attend his funeral, so God was especially good to me this time, even warning me about my mother's death and giving me a song as a guide," Theresa declares.

After her mother's funeral, Theresa and Beth stayed in the United States for two weeks before returning to Brazil. A new year was ready to burst upon them.

"It seemed like I lived in the airplane all of 1974," Bennie recalls. "So many problems arose that required an operational floatplane. At the same time, our own mission was growing rapidly. New works required preaching and teaching visits and to check out building projects. I would spend the night and take off to visit another church the next morning."

He also flew long runs to the extreme points of this huge river system on mercy missions. He has had a man and a woman, both Indians, die on board in flight. He flew to the end of the Demini River once in pouring rain all day with a doctor by his side to help an Indian tribe get their vaccinations and dental work done. On the return flight, the fuel ran out with

145

another hundred yards to go while taxiing on the water to the hangar.

Three or four times Bennie got women out of the jungle with breach birth problems. One fourteen-year-old girl's dead baby protruded from her body while Bennie, his heart aching for the young lady and her agony, guided the plane back to Manaus.

The mayor of Coari, where Bennie was conducting church, came to Bennie with a gruesome request. "Pastor Bennie," he asked, "would you please fly upriver to get the body of a man who has just been murdered?" The body was laid on plastic to prevent the juices that oozed from bullet holes from seeping into the plane, but with the windows open and keeping his nose in the air draft entrance into the plane, Bennie made it back and the family got the remains.

"Pastor Bennie," the FUNAI caller exclaimed, "we have a case of poisonous snakebite at Maral outpost. They radioed us to get him out today if at all possible!"

Two days earlier, an Indian had been working with a machete clearing the jungle nearby when a bushmaster snake (Jara-aka) struck his lower leg. Two small fang holes oozed with something that resembled black ketchup. The leg swelled hideously, and the muscular tissue and skin turned shiny black from the ankle to the knee.

Bennie glanced at his watch. Flying time in the air turtle from Manaus to the Maral outpost requires four and one-half hours, and only three hours of daylight remained. It takes an hour to get to

the floating hangar, gas up, and put the plane in the air ... and floatplanes are not to fly at night.
But ...

After landing on the water and taxiing out of the lake into the serpentine-like creek at the Maral outpost after nightfall, Bennie was ready for a hammock. He consoled himself: *Half the trip is over and there's another day coming at sunrise to finalize this mission.*

Swinging in a hammock is most relaxing when lying in that stretchy cotton bed. One leg bent at the knee and over the side is all the motion needed to create an artificial breeze. It had been a hot, humid day. The gasoline generator purred in a distant shed while a nearly full moon rose in a clear sky. But on the other side of that thatched-roof room in another hammock, the snakebite victim moaned and groaned in pain while Bennie waited for sleep that only came in dots and dashes. At last Bennie rose and walked to the water's edge.

If I can't sleep for the sound of the room, at least I can ready the plane for the flight back to Manaus, Bennie thought. *This will gain time early tomorrow morning.* With his flashlight he made some quick checks under the engine cover and verified the fuel and oil levels.

Stars and a high-rising moon lit the sky. *It's so clear in this moonlight I can read a newspaper,* he thought. Looking at the shining, unruffled lake in the distance, he thought, *With that kind of silvery water and the charcoal black jungle for contrast along its edge, a takeoff or landing would be a piece of cake. It's one beautiful evening, and most of the flight will be over water to Manaus.*

He returned to his hammock, but after another hour of listening to painful moans and pitiful groans from that weakening young man, Bennie pondered a nagging question: "If this were my son in such weakened physical condition and with weather as good as it is for night flying on a trip mostly over water in a seaplane to Manaus and a hospital, would I bend a night-flying restriction to save him or wait out the long night and leave tomorrow with more light and a high probability that he might not be alive twenty-four hours from now?"

So in the moonlight on November 12, 1974, Bennie left Maral with one passenger for Manaus. He had an American night rating for wheel planes that landed easily on lighted runways with bright white lights on each side and blue lights for the taxiways, but water flying is different. However, plenty of water "runways" fanned out in all directions. No one at midnight in the city heard the quiet putter or saw the splashdown of the Cessna 172 on the hotspot of the moon's reflection on the glassy water. The caretaker at the hangar awakened and was curious why such a flight terminated at that late hour. But when he saw the miserable passenger in the back seat of the floatplane, the caretaker agreed that the man was in critical shape.

The two men eased the young patient out of the seat of the plane and slid the hammock under him with minimum contact with the swollen black leg. Bennie hoisted one end of the hammock over his own shoulder, and the caretaker wrapped the other end around his. The patient held the sides with his hands and, swinging the bed, they climbed the riverbank toward Bennie's pickup truck.

The next day Bennie learned from the doctor that the patient's leg was amputated due to gangrene and that the snake-bitten patient's prompt arrival saved his life.

Many times as Bennie walked down a street of Manaus, an unremembered individual approached him and declared that he, a member of his family, or a relative was a passenger in one of Bennie's mercy mission flights and that the situation or health problem would have been far different had Bennie not had the tool for missions work in remote towns on islands, rivers, and lakes of the Amazon Basin. And one of the great follow-up blessings to Bennie's rescue work has been the town mayors who have helped him to acquire and build churches. Even the state governor and his security personnel have trusted their lives to Bennie's skill as a pilot!

Gilberto, a man in demand from both the FUNAI head office in Manaus and Brasilia, the federal capital, gave him a crystal of the frequency of his agency. On December 3, 1974, he asked Bennie to fly from Manaus to the Alalau River.

One never knew what to expect on each flight, but Bennie would not turn down a new adventure even knowing that these same Indians had killed well over a hundred people in their last two generations and a dozen that year. After easing down on the Alalau River a few hundred feet above the present-day concrete bridge that separates the Amazon state from the northern state of Roraima, they taxied to a freshly cut jungle clearing. Felled trees lay all around. After they climbed the bank from the safety of the pontoons of the plane, a group of naked Indians trickled in from the jungle. Bennie wondered as their number constantly increased. Many of those brown men wore only a woven bungee vine wrapped around the waist. They looked strong and carried long, hardened bows that stood above their head. Bennie sensed that Gilberto's smiles didn't quite hide his tenseness. Soon some women appeared, carrying babies or small children in shoulder slings woven from a jungle vine.

"Bennie, this is a fiesta, a party," Gilberto informed him. "We are like invited guests. Don't worry. The women and children here mean there will be no violence."

As some bigger men approached, Bennie smiled and tried to relax, but he knew that he was looking into the face of killers, who only days earlier near this same spot took off with one whack the head of the civilized man who once cooked Bennie's dinner before he crawled into his hammock for the night.

Bennie reached out to one of them, and the Indian lightly shook his hand. They had strong arms and lived by hard work. Some of the men possessed the power and skill to kill alligators or jaguars. As these Indians materialized from the jungle, an amazed Bennie counted 297 of them.

The number he counted that day has always stuck in Bennie's mind. He was concerned to be circled by such a bunch of savage warriors in the heart of the rain forest among towering trees. *Why die in stupidity if I don't have to? Why lose a great life of working for God while I'm still young?* he wondered.

Bennie shrugged the feeling off. Many a missionary would have given anything to do what he was being pulled into doing with these most savage South American tribes. To top it all off, the government agency bought and gave the mission barrels and barrels of aviation fuel that Bennie used to set up their new wave of workers in other remote Amazon River towns.

Smoke drifted upward in the middle of this jungle clearing. The indigenous people motioned them closer to a crude fire burning among the fallen trees. Green stakes with a Y on top were driven into the ground. Other stakes lay across the Y's, and more saplings crossed at right angles to these, forming a grid on which pieces of alligator parts lay with their big scales of leathery green skin. Some long, small pieces of dark meat also were laid over this crude grill. With a start, Bennie recognized that these stringier pieces of meat were monkey. As the naked cook added each new piece, the stench of burning hair filled the atmosphere.

Gilberto, seeing that Bennie was starting to turn away, beckoned for him. "The Indian is preparing this meal, and we must be courteous to eat some of it."

"I already had lunch," Bennie replied. He had—yesterday!

"No, Bennie, be careful; they are all watching. Just eat a little with me," Gilberto cautioned him.

Under the hard scales of the alligator tail, the

white 'gator meat wasn't too bad, but Bennie took longer eating his portion of monkey. The cook had not removed the little hands and fingers. The Indians liked to bite and suck on these well-cooked bits. To finalize the meal, the Indians brought some black bananas.

"They are like jelly!" Bennie protested to Gilberto.

Never missing a beat, he retorted, "You also have to enjoy the dessert!"

Bennie doesn't remember how they eased out of their midst. If any one of the savages was not carrying a big stiff bow and arrows with the sharpened head of a knife filed to a point, he had hidden it nearby under a fallen tree. Bennie and Gilberto did not even have a peashooter, and the Indians knew it. After trying to be friendly, some of them had casually felt their pockets and legs inside their trousers, looking for that possible revolver. Gilberto had some present in the plane to give the chief, but they managed to edge their way to the waiting pontoons of the seaplane and roar away without getting punctured with an arrow. Bennie flew them eighteen minutes further south to the Abonari River outpost, where Gilberto wanted to meet with his pacification crew. He planned to return by foot on the road right-of-way through the jungle to better establish his friendship with this tribe that could move swiftly between these two jungle rivers.

Bennie's mission ended when Gilberto stepped onto the riverbank at Abonari about six miles below the present-day concrete bridge. Bennie well remembers ducking under the left wing strut of the plane as he walked along its pontoon to the front to hand Gilberto the last suitcase of his baggage. Bennie loved the man's dedication and courage; he possessed an inner calmness that in a way reminded Bennie of his father. Gilberto wanted only to see the safe passage of the road through these Indians' territory between Manaus and Boa Vista and was putting his life on the line. He was not deterred from his mission even when others asked him why he would work on such a job, even after losing eleven or twelve of his own men in three massacres in that same area.

"Gilberto," Bennie cautioned, "be very careful. The guys we just left at Alalau can be dangerous! I am not sure I could trust them without their families as we found them by surprise today. You have lost a lot of men this summer in three ambushes that ended as massacres."

"Pastor Bennie," he replied, "had I been here with my men instead of having to go to Brasilia and Manaus for constant meetings and getting supplies, these massacres would not have happened. I know these Indians, and they trust me!"

"They trust me." Those words echoed through Bennie's mind as he stared in unbelief at the Manaus newspaper, *A Noticia*, on Tuesday, December 31, 1974. The biggest, boldest red-ink headlines almost screamed at him: "The Atroaris kill Gilberto."

Stunned, Bennie realized the accompanying photo of Gilberto surrounded by "friendly" Indians was taken just a few days before that fateful Sunday of his death at the river's edge on the Abonari River outpost. He got up early to shave and had gone down to the river to bathe when the signal was given for the attack from the bank above. Eight arrows struck him from behind; three more arrows pierced his body in front after he fell.

It seemed incredible that Gilberto Pinto Figueredo was gone! The same newspaper claimed that he had worked thirty-seven years for FUNAI (National Indian Foundation) and that since 1950 these Indians and many others before killed fifty-eight men. On this massacre, thirty Indians appeared by surprise the night before. Arrows with large, sharp points of knives killed Gilberto with two others, João Monteiro and João Bosco. One had his body opened and his intestines pulled out, and another was thrown in the river to piranhas. Ivã Lima Ferreira, a half-Indian who worked with them, sensed the danger early and had escaped.

A shaken Bennie realized he easily could have been killed with Gilberto. For the time being, he was set back in his hopes to work through this precious, courageous man who was as much home in a modern hotel with government committees as he was in a jungle outpost eating roasted monkey or alligator over an open fire, surrounded by two hundred or more naked, painted Indian warriors.

That year had seen four massacres totaling fourteen deaths by the Atroaris-Waimiris along this federal highway BR-174 between Manaus and Boa Vista. But by faith, Bennie looked ahead to the day when a strong church would arise in this area.

2008 update: Presently the BR-174 highway is asphalted and a wide concrete bridge spans the Alalau River. In nearby areas, Brazilian teachers of Portuguese instruct this tribe in modern schools. They also have medical doctors, nurses, and outposts for medicine, their own buses to the city, video equipment that they use to try to film the white man's damage to the environment, and lawyers to process the government for it.

"Though we have not as a mission made headway with their tribes, God has sent us other tribes that we are slowly reaching," DeMerchant reports. "At the same time we are not breaking any of the many rules about working into these areas where atheist anthropologists form government policy to leave them with their own culture and to keep mission societies out. However, as the tribal peoples move into the cities, these rules are nullified because the Indians meet church people. No one can control that so far."

Some of these men later killed Gilberto.

Wai-Wai Indian children on Mapueira River

Hundreds of children receive the
Holy Ghost at a children's crusade.

The Daredevil
Pentecostal Preacher

"God wants the church to heat up and scorch the devil's hide," Bennie claims. So when he heard of an unconventional minister who had been baptized in Jesus' name and received the revelation of who Jesus is, Bennie asked him to preach a few services in Manaus.

"His methods of working and reaching people were unusual," DeMerchant reports. "Driving through the streets of town, he would use a loudspeaker to announce tremendous healing services at the local church. He even wore different-than-usual attire, a black-and-white checkerboard jacket when in church, and a loose, dark wine-colored cape when having street meetings."

After a few services in Manaus, Bennie decided to fly the man to an Amazonian town far from the capital of Manaus that could be reached quickly only by air travel. The work there needed a boost.

Foreign priests and nuns controlled the city. If one wanted to buy bricks, he was directed to the priest's brick factory. If he wanted lumber, he went to their sawmill. If he wanted mineral water rather than drinking from the parasite and amoeba-infested river, he got water from the church's well and pumping system. For schooling children, friendly nuns taught all the secular subjects and the catechism of the Catholic church. They ran the hospital as well. Three cathedrals offered atonement for the people's souls, and one could pursue an advanced theological career by further study in a convent.

The mayor scarcely dared to move without the counsel of the religious authorities in town lest it be not the religiously correct decision, or in the following election (if he stayed in until then), he and his party lost. This is not a generalization for all cities in Brazil and other Latin American countries where there is purported equality of religion, but often one religion is official and the downtown square must be dedicated to it.

The town where Bennie took his visiting evangelist almost fitted the above description. They had hardly landed in the river before someone of the religious order queried about who they were and what their intentions were. As long as only the faithful few of the church in town congregated quietly and no great group of people attended or showed much interest in the church, no one raised his eyebrows or even paid them much attention.

Bennie's evangelist friend took some passages out of the playbook of those opposed to the gospel message.

"Brother Bennie," he said, "people who have faith in God and come to be healed need a focal point, something to do, as Jesus commanded them. As they obey our Lord's instructions, they'll be healed. Of course, God can do anything anyway He wishes, but He does demand faith and obedience."

To prove his point in a service for healing, the evangelist lined up pop bottles filled with river water that he and the preachers had prayed over. He then commanded the sick to take one bottle home, pray in Jesus' name, and drink the water. For people to receive their healing, rather than praying for each other or having the ministers lay hands on them, the evangelist might ask them to do other things. In many cases his ideas worked and people were healed.

So you guessed it. The two men planned a campaign in their small, wooden local church in the rain forest of the Amazon. God moved. People came to God, and He healed them. Word traveled fast, and the next night the church bulged with people and spilled them onto the street. Folks watched as a deaf and dumb girl opened her mouth and counted with the evangelist, repeating his words to an awed congregation.

The next morning, the two ministers rented a large warehouse, and God moved powerfully the next two nights. He healed people, pitched demons out of them, and filled them with His Spirit. The city began to stir, and in two more days, not even this larger building could hold the crowds.

Therefore, they had to have a larger place in which to preach. Since they were in the dry season, they could have services in the open air. The mayor loaned them sound equipment.

"Just please don't tell anyone I loaned the equipment to you," he pleaded. He enjoyed having someone else in town receiving the usual attacks he did when he opposed these religious, dominating priests.

Bennie stood with the evangelist as he ministered to hundreds of people in the public square in front of city hall. He had commanded them to renounce idolatry and to bring their pictures of saints, their crucifixes, their books of satanic chants, and other relics. When they brought them, he placed the items in a pile and burned them.

In the middle of the week, Bennie flew to another town to minister to an isolated church group needing a visit. When he returned to the daredevil evangelist, the priests swarmed the riverbank to meet him.

"Bennie," they said, "we don't mind you and your people, but you have to get this man you brought with you out of the city!"

While Bennie had been away, these same priests had gone to the local police station and denounced the revival.

"This 'clown' destroys personal property that people held around their necks and pictures of saints on walls, books, and other religious images," they wailed. "He needs to be put in jail."

"I only preach from the Bible," the evangelist countered before the police chief. "Similar things happened in the Book of Acts, chapter nineteen, when people were converted and left their false relics, books, and images and burned them in a pile as I have done. The true church must be fully apostolic and follow the Bible church."

The priests then waved another charge before the police chief.

"This man is no doctor, yet he gave prescriptions for drinking special liquids. That is illegal!" they shrilled.

"I gave the people river water," the evangelist explained. "Anyone can drink it. The ministers present simply prayed over the water. The people can give the water bottles back to you, and you can have it tested. But people were healed, and demons left them."

The angry priests, unable to pin a charge on the evangelist at the police station, left in disgust. They started a campaign warning the townspeople, students in public school, and their church members. "Pastor Bennie and this evangelist teach false doctrine and are ruining the official religion that has worked smoothly for years," they trumpeted. "And they are not friends of Our Lady, the Virgin Mary."

Meanwhile, the chief of police, hearing that the evangelist was praying and that people were getting healed, asked, "Would you come with me to my house to pray for my sick wife?"

God healed his wife in such a manner that the delighted chief of police ordered two armed soldiers in uniform to accompany Bennie and the evangelist to any public meeting until they left town! Eyes followed their every move wherever they walked during the day. They handed out lots of tracts and attracted people with their portable, battery-operated speaker system.

One day, Bennie removed the right door from the airplane and they took off, loaded with tracts and with the speaker blaring. Climbing to a safe altitude over the suburbs of the town, Bennie cut back on the throttle and semi-glided in slow circles while the evangelist turned up the loud-speaker to full blast, announcing the "largest ever evangelical church meeting in town in front of city hall on the square!" They repeated this over several suburbs.

When time came to start the meeting in the square, one couldn't push a bicycle through the dense crowd. The sound system was up and going. To be seen, Bennie and the evangelist stood on concrete benches. Windows on ground level and above sported bodies and heads of onlookers who eyed their every move. The evangelist preached about Jesus and how He healed people.

"At the end of the meeting, you'll have an opportunity to be prayed for," he promised the crowd. "By the name of Jesus, demons can be cast out, so if anyone is afflicted by demons or evil spirits, bring those folks to the front."

Later, several persons were brought forward, and in the name of Jesus, their violent manifestations stopped.

Then a priest elbowed his way through the crowd. Angrily pointing his finger at the evangelist, he turned and shouted, "This is not of God. This is the work of these 'clowns of the devil'!"

He screamed this over and over, his face getting red. The whole crowd became silent. No one dared question the word of the priest. The evangelist, clutching the microphone, pointed at another woman they were bringing for prayer. She was writhing and hissing like a snake.

"I command you, Satan, to come out of this woman and enter this priest who night after night has come here to trouble us in these meetings!" the evangelist boldly stated.

The last Bennie saw of the priest was his back as he scooted down the street with his student protesters.

The meeting continued. It was Bennie's turn to minister. The daredevil evangelist passed him the microphone. The whole multitude surged forward. The two uniformed police officers stood sternly by their side, alert to the grumblings of the crowd. Then the large crowd hushed. Instantly, without missing a beat, a complete sermon flooded Bennie's mind. He preached hard for an hour under a boldness he had rarely felt in his life!

His sermon thoughts, already ignited by the organized, priest-led march that denounced them repeatedly as not being friends of Our Lady, flared to bonfire proportions.

"We are the greatest friends of Our Lady, the Virgin Mary," Bennie proclaimed. "We follow her advice in John, chapter two; she ordered the servants to do whatever Jesus said. 'Whatsoever He says unto you, do it!' His mother said."

Bennie had a pile of fun standing in front of that huge crowd, preaching what Jesus said about repentance, baptism, and reception of the Holy Ghost.

"If you follow the steps of Our Lady, they will bring you to a church that seeks and receives the Holy Ghost as she did on the Day of Pentecost," he concluded.

Some business folk of the town came to him afterward and exclaimed, "We were beginning to fear for you, Pastor Bennie! Things were developing that looked bad. We watched from the upper windows of the building. You have a great education, and it got you out of a situation that was going bad!"

That, Bennie thought, *was their way of saying it, but to me the education was God.*

After the service Bennie asked the evangelist, "Why would you cast those demons out of that twisting woman and into the priest?"

"I've had my fill of that priest all week," he retorted. "I've met him on the street. He was at the police station, too. I knew he was full of the devil, and if a few more evil spirits entered him, it wouldn't make any difference."

When the two preachers roared full throttle on the lake into liftoff, they had had a week of reliving the Book of Acts. God had helped them in their weak ways to present Him to unsaved souls. These meetings encouraged the local church so much that it became widely known for its bold and aggressive proclamation of truth.

2008 update: Nine more churches and a good Bible school thrive in that town that has graduated over a hundred trained workers and is also a district headquarters to thirty-five other churches out of town on the river that runs through the rain forest and reaches into three Indian tribal areas.

He Maketh Me to Lie Down

Around the beginning of 1975, Bennie purchased a small Honda motorbike. He and Theresa had been having prayer meetings in the evenings with some of their church people in a lowland semi-jungle area where the property owner had a thatch-roofed, open-sided building with a concrete floor. Moreover, the place was quiet and cool after sunset. Although the owner was friendly to the group, Bennie always asked his permission to use the facility. However, the owner lacked a telephone. Since the place was just north of town, Bennie mounted the "Honda 70" and zipped his way to north Manaus. The group wanted to use the location for a prayer meeting that night.

As Bennie topped a hill leaving the city, a bus ahead of him discharged dense puffs of black, evil-smelling diesel fumes. At the top of the hill, the street leveled out, and Bennie accelerated the bike to pass the bus on the left. Suddenly the bus driver swerved sharply to the left to avoid a stretch of potholes. Bennie, beside the bus, did not see the potholes. The bus driver, intent on avoiding the potholes as much as possible, did not see Bennie.

The long metallic side of the bus slammed into Bennie's right leg. The bus caught the motorcycle by a footrest, swung it under the rear axle, and spewed it out the back. The pavement rushed up at Bennie, and he saw stars as his helmet hit the ground and rolled down the street.

The driver never stopped.

As a result of this unequal tangle, Bennie lay in Saint Lucas hospital in Manaus, his collarbone broken, his right leg snapped in three places, and a thick peppering of road rash on his face and shoulder. After ten days Dr. Mangueira reluctantly released Bennie to go home, but the concerned doctor called daily to verify that Bennie was on the mend and was doing arm exercises to get his shoulder mobile. Bennie hobbled around the house on crutches.

As Bennie recovered, he continued preaching in the churches in Manaus, sitting in a chair with his plaster-cast leg angled to the floor and his toes protruding from the cuff of his trousers.

Almost two months passed. Bennie figured it was time to take to the air again. He calculated that he could place his right foot on the copilot's side on a small block of wood. Besides, he operated most of the main controls by hand. So with a wide river and calm water on July 11, 1975, he took off solo to see how he could handle the floatplane with one foot free for using on the rudders. After several takeoffs and landings, it was just a matter of getting used to the amount of pressure needed for his one usable foot, and he soon nailed down the technique.

The Lord had made him lie down ... but only for a little while. It was time for another furlough and another stretch of deputation travel. Missionaries Mark and Eunice Norris arrived in Manaus from Rio de Janeiro to assume the responsibility for the work around Manaus as the DeMerchants deputized in North America for a year that started at the end of July 1975.

On a windy fall afternoon in Collinsville, Illinois, where the DeMerchants were undergoing two weeks of retraining, Bennie heard the propeller putter of a Cessna plane overhead. Holding to his crutches, he looked up as a new Cessna 206 land plane circled and dropped nicely into the Willamancette Christian Center's open field. Bennie's friend Gerald Grant hopped from the cockpit. He had completed an order by the Foreign Missions Board: "Buy and equip a new and much larger Cessna floatplane for Bennie in Brazil and fly it into this campground for an afternoon dedication."

After the dedication in Illinois, Grant flew the plane back to Saint Paul, where it would be mounted on PK3500 floats that would carry almost twice the load of the smaller Cessna 172.

After a school year of deputation work in 1975-76 in North America, the DeMerchants tarried in Perth, New Brunswick, Canada, until the arrival of their third child on August 8, 1976, a son they named Bennie Jonas.

Bennie asked Clayton Goodine, a longtime friend and owner of a Piper Pacer seaplane, to accompany him and eleven-year-old Beth on ferrying the Cessna 206 to Brazil. Thus, on August 20, the three of them took to the skies after goodbyes from Theresa, seven-year-old Pam, the new baby boy, and a collection of relatives and local church folk. This powerful bird began its hop-hop flight to Brazil. They arrived in Manaus on August 28, three days ahead of heart-wrenching tragedy.

The Cessna 206 seaplane

Extinguished Candles

Phone calls welcoming Bennie back to Brazil jangled the phone constantly. One caller invited him to visit Maués, 165 miles east of Manaus.

"Pastor Bennie, five churches in the area are having a fellowship rally on August 31. Will you come?"

Of course he would! Bennie was delighted to be back in Brazil, and this invitation afforded him the opportunity to get up to date on not one but five churches! He would take Clayton, Beth, and Sister Margaret.

Sister Margaret, who had been teaching in the Bible school in Rio, was filling in the thirty-day time gap between the departure of the Mark Norris family from Rio de Janeiro, who had supervised the DeMerchants' work in Manaus for nearly a year but had to return to Rio before Bennie's return, and his arrival. Sister Margaret wanted to get back to Rio and was scheduled to leave on the Monday after Bennie and company arrived Saturday from Canada with the new airplane.

Early on the morning of the anticipated flight to Maués, someone clapped his hands at the door. It was Jose Cinque, a young single man who graduated from the Bible school in Rio and had spent over a year in the beginnings of the distant church on the Juruá River in Eirunepé. A suitcase dangled from his right hand.

"Pastor Bennie," he said, "I would go with you to Maués."

"Jose, you just got a new job!" Bennie exclaimed. "You better stick with the new job lest the manager at the hotel dismiss you. There will be other opportunities to visit Maués."

"Oh, no, Pastor Bennie," Jose hurried to explain. "My manager is allowing me to go."

Bennie took Beth aside. "Beth, would you stay here? After all, you've had enough floatplane flying from Canada to Brazil. Would you give your place to Jose?"

A crestfallen Beth reluctantly agreed, for she had eagerly anticipated being with Sister Margaret for the day.

So on Tuesday afternoon at about 2 o'clock, Bennie, Clayton, Sister Margaret, and Jose buckled themselves inside the new plane for a visit to this area southeast of Manaus.

As they climbed into the plane, Sister Margaret stepped back a moment to admire it. "Brother Bennie," she said, "this plane is so huge and new, it should last for many years of good service."

Bennie water-taxied the Cessna 206 floatplane N-35502 at the mouth of Taraumã Creek toward Rio Negro Bay. But while Bennie and Clayton checked and readied the plane to go full throttle in this, the new plane's first missions flight, the sky darkened over the city eight miles to the east as a rain shower and its accompanying ground wind approached.

Beyond the trees on the point of land ahead and to the right lay a body of water fourteen miles long. The wind lashed its surface into six-foot waves, but where the plane floated in the sheltered cove, the water was only slightly choppy.

The plane lifted into the air. To avoid the squall then about four miles away, Bennie circumnavigated it to the south and banked the plane in a right turn toward the bay at about one hundred feet of altitude. He was talking with the microphone to the control tower when without warning the engine abruptly stopped.

The plane was turned with its wings perpendicular to the big waves. At its low altitude, Bennie had no room to turn back straight into the wind. He was in a dreaded crosswind situation with no power. The little altitude he had was bleeding away fast! He hit the emergency fuel pump switch. The fuel pump snarled as the whine of the propeller diminished. As Bennie rounded out of the glide above the waves, the three-bladed propeller stopped completely. The pontoons squashed on the water parallel with the high waves.

This is definitely the wrong way to land a seaplane in a strong crosswind, Bennie thought.

171

He knew it was a freak occurrence when altitude would not allow the plane to land straight into the wind and bounce on the rough waves with maximum lowered wing flaps for a slow touchdown.

Bennie used the ailerons to the maximum to hold down the left wing to balance the plane as much as possible. A mountainous black wave surged in from the left. He glanced at the right wing tip as it neared the water and knew what would happen when it struck. He grabbed the V bar in the windshield. He was helpless to control the effects of the wind as that wing struck the water.

No one spoke a word. Absolute silence filled the aircraft.

The water grabbed the wing and cartwheeled the plane. It landed upside down in the river. Immediately, water rushed in and completely flooded the cabin. The impact jammed the flaps of the wing against the two double doors on the right side of the plane where Sister Margaret and Jose were sitting.

Underwater, Bennie reached around and three different times grabbed the door handle and twisted it to force this door open. It would not budge.

The old Cessna 172 had a small baggage door behind all seats. Thinking of this, Bennie swam quickly inside the water-filled cabin to the rear baggage area. Some floating suitcases blocked his view as he groped in vain for such a baggage-door latch on this new plane. Bennie was a strong swimmer and could hold his breath over a minute under water, but he realized that he was trapped inside the rear of this plane.

In the murk, he spotted a little plastic, trapezoid-shaped window about his size.

He pounded it three or four times with his fist. The center part of it finally broke, leaving jagged pieces of plastic protruding from its edges. Ignoring damage to his fist, he struck the window several times until he was able to get his head and shoulders out. His shirt ripped as he struggled through. But the small opening held him fast around his belt line.

Bennie was trapped and by then taking in water. His mind raced. He could go no further and needed air. His whole past life and call to the Amazon flashed before him.

Jesus! Help me get clear of this wreckage under this river. I want to see many more churches come to existence in the Amazon! his heart cried. At that point he kicked hard and felt his thighs and knees scrape through the window!

He was free. He reached the light on the surface and between high waves gulped in air and looked around. He saw only the bottoms of the pontoons of the submerged aircraft with its wing shadow underneath. As the banana-like pontoons dived into a wave and emerged on the other side, Bennie spotted the head of his front seat passenger, Clayton Goodine, who had also somehow escaped.

Where were the heads of the other two? They could not be seen in the water.

A speedboat containing five or six men bounced on the waves and stopped beside the overturned aircraft. On the beach a few hundred feet away, they had witnessed it all.

"Two people are still in the plane!" Bennie yelled.

The men, already wearing swimming trunks, dived down each side of the plane and resurfaced several times.

"We can't get inside!" they yelled, and dived again and again.

Too weak to do much more than gulp air, a desperate Bennie urged the men on.

"We'll give these folks mouth-to-mouth resuscitation," he promised.

After half an hour, the men claimed it was useless to continue. They tied a rope from the boat to the submerged plane and towed it very slowly upside down toward shallower water.

By then the fire department had arrived. The rescuers pried open the plane and got the two drenched bodies of Sister Margaret and Jose out of the aircraft and lay them on a boat ramp, where Clayton and Bennie sat waiting for the police and other authorities to arrive. That wait seemed like an eternity to Bennie.

The next three days kaleidoscoped into chaos for Bennie. The coroners took the bodies, examined them, and announced that Sister Margaret and Jose had drowned. On September 1, 1976, headlines blazoned the accident of the United Pentecostal Church's floatplane. The newspaper published bizarre photographs of the drowned passengers, the wrecked plane with wings pushed back, the sad and aging parents of Jose, and Bennie and Clayton in shock at the scene.

The nightmare accident happened so unexpectedly and at the only critical time of the flight. With only two hundred feet more of altitude, Bennie could have executed a sharp left turn and made a landing straight into the wind. From that point to Maués, the entire trip would have been either over or within gliding range of the natural waterports of smaller lakes and rivers if an engine failed.

Over the next seventy-two hours, Bennie received visits from aeronautical officials and fielded national and international phone calls. He preached Jose's funeral. During the same time, he completed the paperwork for the release to ship Sister Margaret's remains to the United States for a funeral later preached in Indianapolis by Brother Nathaniel A. Urshan.

The phone rang constantly, the doorbell incessantly, and church folks offered sympathy continuously. Clayton and Beth were with Bennie during those harrowing days, but Goodine, with English as his sole language, could only help and encourage Bennie. Once Bennie wandered around downtown, unable to remember where he parked his car. Fortunately, Clayton had accompanied him and helped him find the vehicle. Theresa, Bennie's stay and always-solid support, had not returned yet from Canada with Pamela and Bennie Jr.

The media turned vicious. Some creative reporter wrote articles accusing Bennie of willfully crashing the plane for insurance purposes. He condemned Bennie with dreamed-up quotes in Portuguese that Bennie had supposedly made, using words Bennie never used in Portuguese. Another newspaper's sub-headlines stated of the Americans and Brazilians: United in Death!

What betrayal! Bennie had used his mission seaplane and risked his life to save many other lives, flying trips for thousands of miles with medical supplies, doctors and nurses, heart attack and snakebite victims. Now, that lifesaving work was obliterated by the sensation-stalking media.

But the cruelest comment of all came from one of the prominent members (who had caused some trouble in times past in the church) of the central church in Manaus, who sidled up to Bennie as Bennie gazed into Jose's casket in front of the pulpit.

"Pastor Bennie," he declared, "the hand of God is against you. You must close down and leave Brazil very soon. Our churches will never grow nor get over this. God is against you, so your mission will dry up and blow away."

Bennie staggered at this callous comment. In the confusion that ensued after the accident, he had worked hard for three long, twenty-four-hour days and was worn out physically. Sleep escaped him. The scene replayed itself in his mind over and over when he closed his eyes. At night, he could only lie in bed and weep, sobbing uncontrollably through the long night until dawn finally broke and people appeared.

The loss of two lives weighed heavily on Bennie. His head drooped low. Upon his shoulders rested the deaths of two young people who had been so instrumental in the work of God. Exhausted and knocked flat on his face, he thought, *If one day there ever will be a strong, widespread Pentecostal church in northern Brazil, it will be God's work and not mine.*

Bennie tossed sleeplessly on his bed in their home in Manaus. In the early hours of September 3, he wept and prayed earnestly as he questioned God. "Why, why, why, Lord, would You allow this to happen when it seemed the future was so bright?"

Suddenly a tall man in white appeared in the door of the room. He approached Bennie, turned sideways, and slightly bent his shoulders. He looked down at Bennie as he placed his hand firmly on Bennie's shoulder.

"Have I not called you to this country to preach the gospel? I am pilot-in-command of your life! Get up and go on with the work. I will bless you and the work as never before!"

He turned and went out the door.

Calmness and relief swept over Bennie. A tremendous load lifted. He felt light on his feet and even giddy in believing what that man told him. Fearlessness buoyed him. He knew that thousands had heard of the accident and were praying for them, but this incident engraved itself permanently in his mind.

The sun rode high in the morning when Bennie awoke. He immediately told Clayton what had occurred during the night.

"Bennie, in all my life I have never seen you so low," he replied.

And an amazing thing happened. Bennie's preaching became bold and very positive. People noticed and commented that he had definitely changed and had a very positive outlook for the work and his ministry in general. All in Manaus knew of the happenings of that fateful day of August 31,

1976, when disaster left him devastated, but God, in His great mercy, turned despair to victory.

The Lord did not leave Bennie comfortless. Before long, he heard two testimonies that showed him God held the whole accident in His hands. Brother Stephen Baker, a missionary in southern Brazil, told Bennie later in a fellowship meeting that God showed him that something serious would happen to Sister Margaret in Manaus and told her so before she got her ticket and left Rio.

Jose had received a warning, too. The young man, visiting the church in Marrecão, preached and then joined them in prayer meeting when a man got up and walked to where he was kneeling.

Placing his hand on Jose's shoulder, the man asked, "Jose, are you ready to meet Jesus soon?"

"Yes," Jose answered firmly.

"Very soon you will be with Him, so be ready!"

A month later, after prayer, Bennie wrote a letter to the Foreign Missions Board and gave them an update of his situation since the accident. He proposed three options:

> 1) I am willing to forget about flying altogether and work with our people and use boats on the rivers;
> 2) We can keep our little, old Cessna 172 float-plane going and keep on using it;
> 3) The Cessna 206 floatplane that crashed has been totaled and is beyond repair. We can salvage some things to sell for debts or hold them on hand if another of the same type is purchased, and continue with our original plan before the accident.

To Bennie's surprise, his great friend Gerald Grant in Saint Paul, Minnesota, who had helped purchase and equip Bennie's two previous seaplanes, phoned him.

"Bennie, the Foreign Missions Board has met and decided. They will authorize the purchase of a replacement aircraft, and you will go on with the original plan!"

At the end of September 1976, the whole fellowship sadly paid tribute to Sister Margaret at General Conference with thousands of ministers and members present. The news of the deaths of Sister Margaret in the United States and of Jose Cinque in Brazil stirred many of the young ministers to step into the work to fill their place wherever God called them, regardless of the sacrifice they might make one day.

Over the ensuing years, busloads from 125 churches in the Manaus area have driven to that same beach where the accident happened to have church and baptize hundreds of believers, with a dozen ministers baptizing folks in Jesus' name in one setting. How great is our God!

Margaret Calhoun, victim of
plane crash near Manaus
August 31, 1976

Evangelizing with Leo Upton

After the disaster of the Cessna 206 floatplane Bennie did not fly again for almost two months. His faithful little Cessna 172 floated securely in the floating hangar in the Taruamã River cove. Eventually he stirred up the courage to fly again. In October he visited the Autazes church that Sister Margaret and Jonas started five years earlier with her flannelboard and children's stories, and touched down at several more churches on the rivers and lakes that due to his long furlough needed looking after.

The Foreign Missions Division wrote Bennie about the possibility of scheduling special meetings in northern Brazil with someone of whom he had heard but had not met, Brother Leo Upton. Bennie gave the green light to the whole suggestion.

Brother Upton was close to seventy years old when he first came to Manaus. A slim, elderly man,

Brother Upton was both genial and humble, and a fount of wisdom in many areas of church administration. He had been a denominational minister who did not believe that a believer spoke in tongues when he or she received the Holy Ghost. But his own open heart and his sincerity in prayer brought the Pentecostal experience into his life and revolutionized his ministry. Later he joined the United Pentecostal Church International as a minister and still later applied for overseas work as a missionary evangelist. He spent the rest of his days bringing this experience he had opposed to as many as possible wherever he went. His kind, elderly wife understood that and waited and prayed at home for his success and safe return from weeks abroad.

A man of tremendous sincerity, simplicity, and stamina, Brother Upton stayed in the apartment that had been built for Sister Margaret and prayed there many hours. His sermons created such a hunger in his listeners that the altars filled with seekers in a short time.

In one service in Santo Antonio, the pastor confirmed that seventeen of those present had not received the Holy Ghost and that ten of these were just good old folks who never missed a service or caused any problem but at the same time never really got serious enough to receive this experience.

Following Brother Upton's instructions on how to receive the Holy Ghost, the service that started quietly built to such a crescendo that it seemed the roof of the building could blow off at any time! At the close of that service, all seventeen had received the Holy Ghost—including the ten chronic seekers.

Bennie talked Brother Upton into going to spend the night at a fine, elderly Pentecostal couple's rural home a hop from Manaus in the seaplane.

"We can get up early and catch some peacock bass," was the lure Bennie dangled in front of Brother Upton.

The duo arrived just before sunset. The Brazilian couple claimed that they had received this experience, but before long, Bennie and Brother Upton discovered that they had not been baptized into the name of Jesus for remission of sins. Before going to their hammocks that night, they showed the couple verses of Scripture they could read aloud in the Book of Acts.

"This is the way the apostles baptized believers," the two preachers explained. "After they themselves received the Holy Ghost, they realized that the 'name' in Matthew 28:19 is Jesus."

As the sun started to rise the next morning, Bennie stood in the water beside the pontoon of the seaplane and baptized this fine, hardworking couple in Jesus' name. Then he and Brother Upton trolled the lake awhile, not having missed a night with "something to do" for His kingdom, even while on an overnight outing!

Bennie and Brother Upton shared some great experiences. They had a tight schedule of ministering in the upper Juruá River, where the large mother church was located in the city of Eirunepé. On the narrow, crooked Eiru River, congregations had already been established, but many such groups were unable to attend services in Eirunepé for a variety of reasons. One such body of believers sent for Bennie to visit one of their preaching points the next day, which was Sunday. The two preachers needed to be in the church in Eirunepé that night but had a brief slot of time left for a quick house meeting in the afternoon.

As Bennie flew over the winding, narrow Eiru River, Brother Upton looked down.

"Are you landing on that narrow jungle river?" he asked, his voice tense.

"Yes," Bennie responded. "It's short and narrow, but I have been in and out of here on previous trips."

"I believe I'd rather parachute down and from the ground watch you land," Brother Upton said.

Brother Upton shut his eyes as Bennie threaded the plane exactly in the middle of the narrow slot between tall cypress trees overhanging the river. Tree limbs wisped the wings of the landing bird, and soon the men climbed from the plane and tied up in front of a house made of thatch.

Twenty-seven people had packed into this small building. It was very hot outside and breathlessly so inside. Brother Upton preached. The Holy Ghost didn't mind that so many were crowded in the heat! The Holy Ghost fell on these people one by one until all twenty-seven had received a powerful experience with God.

With great satisfaction, Bennie pushed the throttle all the way in, and they roared away, through the trees and to the city for a great service there that Sunday night. Future ministers from the area would remember that powerful service for years to come.

"Where are we flying to today?" Brother Upton was always eager to go.

"Two hundred miles east of Manaus," Bennie replied, and they flew there.

The local church people had worked hard to prepare for the arrival of the visiting ministers. They had built an open-sided shelter that was covered with thatch. Pots of beans and rice simmered for an after-service meal. However, as people were praying and receiving the Holy Ghost at the altar, hecklers surrounded the church and yelled through the windows at those who were praying. They went to the pots of food and strewed their contents around the building on the ground.

Seeing all the commotion outside, a tall, timid, elderly man named Brother Noah had quit praying. Investigation soon confirmed that the pots were empty. Brother Upton and Bennie knew it was useless in this atmosphere to try to continue. But Brother Upton had seen Noah's earnest desire for the Holy Ghost.

"We will have an early prayer service at five o'clock tomorrow morning and get up before the devil does," Brother Upton announced. The church agreed. And in the early-morning meeting, Noah received his great experience in the Holy Ghost.

Bennie and Brother Upton left that place with great joy and satisfaction because people did receive the baptism of the Holy Ghost in spite of the loss of the food. The two preachers agreed that the fulfillment of the spiritual hunger far supplanted that of the natural hunger. Best of all, elderly Noah had been the final one to receive the Holy Ghost in the early-morning meeting.

At least two years passed before Brother Upton and Bennie again visited that church on the lake. Upon landing, they learned that Noah had died just an hour earlier.

What if we had not scheduled that second meeting? Bennie mused. *That decision Brother Upton made could have made a difference in eternity for dear Brother Noah.*

In Brother Upton's three trips to Manaus over a period of about four to five years and flying with Bennie to far-flung flocks all over the Amazon, more than a thousand souls received the baptism of the Holy Ghost. Several of the present-day ministers in those areas look back to those services under the Holy Ghost spout! Thus the foundation of a strong church in northern Brazil was laid, and leaders for further growth and revival needed to be trained quickly.

The wave of the Holy Ghost and the training of those left in its wash would structure this growing church that Bennie and Theresa hoped would reach all over Brazil and strengthen the scattered works they and other missionaries already had started.

Did not the Lord advise Bennie on September 3, 1976, after the terrible plane crash, that He was pilot-in-command and that if Bennie got up and went on with the work He would bless it?

God was standing by His word!

More would come!

Leave This to Me!

"Frame this letter and leave it to Me!"

Bennie thought he heard this small inner voice as he stared at a certificate from the Brazilian licensing board that ordered him to fly the new Cessna 206 out of the country. If Bennie didn't comply, the Brazilian government would confiscate the plane.

The easiest part of operating an airplane is flying it. The paperwork and logistics of refueling, importing, maintenance, and taxes are part of the heavy yoke that any pilot or aircraft owner must bear to stay in the air. The Brazilian government dropped this yoke on Bennie's neck and then screwed it tight.

In the early morning of October 17, 1977, more than thirteen months after the accident, Bennie and [the late] Brother Wayne Rooks had circled the new Cessna 206 seaplane above Brother Rook's precious wife Trudy as she shielded her squinting eyes in the Miami morning sun and watched until the plane was out of sight. Well equipped with navigational and communication radios, the plane ferried the men to Brazil in six days.

Bennie and Brother Rooks had arrived in Brazil flying the new plane under a temporary foreign permit that in six months would expire. As in the previous importation process to nationalize the floatplane, the new plane needed a release from customs. The church also had to be registered with governmental social assistance organs that exempted taxes if the donation of the plane were to be received and nationalized under the auspices of the Brazilian church.

Brazil started producing its own single-engine airplanes to avoid expensive imports and to modernize its fleets by using national labor at lower costs. But Brazil did this after Bennie had imported the first Cessna 172. Although half of Brazil lies in the Amazon Basin and is a natural "Tropical Alaska" for growth and development, all Brazilian planes were made for land operations and the door was slammed shut for the water birds to be imported. This changeover affected the importation of Bennie's new plane.

To the Brazilian way of thinking, Bennie would be flying in the largest standing forest of the world and in an area where evasive drug-running aircraft also operated. To release an aircraft that could take off and land on narrow stretches of water was to grant permission for it to go in and out of millions of uncontrolled places and might even be operating under a religious front.

The importation board turned down Bennie's request to legally import the plane. Bennie offered even more documentation of his assistance work. Friends inside the government promised help.

The board refused their request a second time.

Bennie renewed the temporary license. When it expired, he renewed it again. Then the plane's annual inspection, issued from an approved maintenance shop in the United States, also expired. No approved maintenance shop in Brazil dared brave the Brazilian government and work on the plane. The United States registered plane needed to be given an annual inspection by a licensed United States aviation mechanic. Fortunately, an American Baptist Mid-Missions missionary pilot, Robert Lankford, who had a mechanic's license with the FAA, inspected the plane, giving it a fresh annual for twelve months of flying, thus legalizing the use of it anywhere in the world! Whether imported or not, this needed to be done to fly back to the United States, and Bennie's regional director, [the late] Brother Paul Leaman told him to do so ASAP.

To fight through the importation dilemma, Bennie called in an army of prayer warriors: the saints in Brazil; their partners in missions; and General Superintendent Nathaniel A. Urshan, who knew of the problem and even contacted his Indiana senator, Richard Lugar.

"Theresa, if we ever get this faster and much larger aircraft imported into Brazil as its permanent home after all we have tried, it will be an act of God!" Bennie declared. They were stymied on every side.

Then God acted. Big time. But then, He's a big-time God!

189

Here is how God solved the problem: In Coroado, their largest church in Manaus, a fellowship meeting was closing when a large car with a lady candidate for senator and her entourage drove up and stopped. She entered the building. The congregation, which had started to leave, returned from outside.

"What is your greatest need?" she asked.

"We need Pastor Bennie's plane cleared for importation!" the ministers replied.

"I'll take care of that," she guaranteed, and after some greetings and friendly discussion, she left. She followed up her promise by sending a close friend to the DeMerchant's home in Manaus to hear of the problem.

"If you can help us, we can help the lady in her campaign," Bennie promised. "It will take sixty hours of flight time to return the plane to the United States and then import it back into Brazil. If the plane doesn't have to leave Brazil, I will use those sixty hours to fly the candidate up and down the Amazon."

The candidate's aide left with the documentation in hand. After all, Bennie's mission now numbered eight thousand votes!

A few days later, Bennie received a telephone call to appear with the head of his mission in Brazil, Brother Robert Norris, at this lady senator's office in Brasilia. She had turned Bennie's documents over to the President of Brazil. He had given the papers to the Minister of Aeronautics, who controls all military and civil aviation in the country.

Brother Norris from Rio and Bennie

DeMerchant from the Amazon arrived by different airlines in Brasilia. The lady senator and her chauffer in an official government car accompanied the two men to the Ministry of Aeronautics building. With her, the two missionaries quickly passed security and took an elevator to the top floor, where they stepped into a huge, plush office with large glass windows giving a panoramic view of that part of Brasilia. Bennie and Brother Norris sat quietly while the senator with documentation and request in hand approached the elderly minister.

"This mission has a Cessna 172 on floats that they have been using several years in church, rescue, and assistance work in the Amazon region of our country," she explained. "They need a larger plane for water operations. This mission has over eight thousand adults who attend their churches."

"The standard procedure is to turn down requests to import any single-engine aircraft because we make our own," the minister stated. "There must be an overwhelming reason for approval, and the mission must verify their activities in the country, especially in this northern area. FUNAI must also approve the process."

Before Bennie and Brother Norris left, the minister promised that the import request would be re-examined and they would be given the final word.

That word came a few days later when a certified letter from the same board, which had turned them down twice, stated that in view of the minister's request they had approved the importation of the new Cessna 206 to Brazil.

Oh, praise and jubilation!

When Bennie presented this documented approval to Brazilian customs, he was surprised that customs did not respond for several days.

Then Bennie's customs dispatch agent called. "The customs officers want to meet you at their executive suite on the top of the customs building in downtown Manaus," he said.

Bennie and the dispatching agent met with those executives. When Bennie and the agent entered, the customs officials all rose, greeted Bennie, and shook his hand.

They had seen the letter of approval but thought it was false, so they had delayed. No one wanted to make any mistake. Only after communication exchanges with government organs in Brasilia did Manaus customs confirm and move further on this.

"We couldn't believe what had happened, and we wanted to meet you," the officials said. "This is not only a day of festival, Pastor Bennie, of getting authorization for your seaplane to be imported into Brazil, but also of being exempted of over fifty-seven thousand dollars of import taxes! Your aircraft comes into Brazil duty-free."

How were those officials to know that other Brazilian officials would soon be knocking at Bennie's door, asking for his help using the new seaplane?

Hitchhiking Dogs and Flying Pigs

Bennie and Pastor Jonas splashed down in the Cessna floatplane on the Autazes River to visit Jonas's uncle and aunt, who owned a cattle farm near the jungle. Two dogs cavorted around the pastors with friendly barks and wagging tails when the men stepped out of the floatplane.

The top of the Edo aluminum floats had black, sandpaper-like rectangular patches that prevented slipping. As the men ended their visit and entered the plane, both dogs jumped on a pontoon. One fell off. The other gained more solid footing on the rough rubber surface.

The engine of the plane was running when Bennie turned into the wind. When he looked outside, he saw that the dog still clung to the rear of the pontoon. Not wanting to stop the engine and knowing well that the dogs often swam in the river to avoid the heat, Bennie decided to take off.

With his slippery toenails on the float, he'll be soon gone in the wind as we pick up speed, and he'll swim back home, Bennie thought. He paid no further attention to the dog until the plane had reached an altitude of about two hundred feet.

When Bennie looked back at the rear of the float, he was astonished at what he saw! The dog had squatted flat and managed to get a front shoulder and leg behind a diagonal strut that descended from the front of the fuselage to the pontoon. There he hung, his head low and ears flopping backward in the wind. Bennie's immediate reaction was to circle with the seaplane, return to the starting point, and restore the dog to its owner or in the river nearby. However, as he thought of it, he realized he would fly over jungle in the turn.

If the dog got loose or afraid by the bank of the plane in the turn, he would fall into the woods and be killed, Bennie thought.

The river was still underneath, so Bennie cut power, dropped the flaps, and flew straight ahead. He eased the plane back onto the water. Stopping and stepping onto the pontoon, he untangled the animal from the strut. The dog plunged into the river and paddled furiously toward the riverbank.

Several years later, Bennie remembered what he had learned from the hitchhiking dog when he had a similar adventure with a far different kind of animal.

Within a few years after the death of Gilberto, who worked so diligently to pacify the Atroari-Wairimi Indians, the road wound through their reserve and connected Boa Vista, the capital of Roraima, to

Manaus, the capital of Amazonas. It was still a tense time, but the government did everything in its power to satisfy the basic health, food, and educational needs of these jungle tribes. Children needed vaccinations and boosters. Like all people, Indians had their times when someone fell sick, had a complicated childbirth, got snake bitten, or suffered other accidents. They learned that the white man could help them.

With the road opened, the FUNAI folks operated a halfway house for the Indians on the road to Itacoatiara, out of town about twelve miles going northeast. There, with nurses and basic medicines to tend to any sick people or anyone who needed more complicated medical help, the Indians could hang their hammocks. Later the FUNAI workers would load the Indians into a Volkswagon van and drive the Indians around the city to different stores, where they were able to buy clothing and other needs. The Indians who live constantly in the green rain forest like the colors of things they do not see, especially bright red. They also like knives, machetes, axes, fishing lines, mirrors, and hairpieces. They learned to use toothbrushes, toothpaste, soap, and towels and to launder their clothes with powdered soap—after they started wearing clothes.

Bennie was asked to fly to the FUNAI outpost on the Curiau River with a doctor, nurse, and vaccines to attend to the Indians' basic health needs. Thirty days later, the medical team would return to give booster shots.

After some hours of work in the morning, Dr. Irineu and his nurse were ready to take off for Manaus. But the doctor had one problem. A poisonous snake had bitten the ten-year-old son of the chief, and his leg was black around the bite.

"We've treated that snakebite wound, but I fear that gangrene could set in and the leg would have to be amputated," the doctor said. "We need to take him to the hospital in Manaus."

So the youngster was carried into the aircraft.

Before getting onboard, Dr. Irineu called Bennie aside.

"Pastor Bennie, I have a problem and need your opinion," the doctor said in a low voice. "The chief's son needs proper specialized attention with this leg, and his father gave me the best kind of a present they offer friends. It is a live wild pig. I have an area behind my house and can pen it there if we can get it to Manaus. Would it be possible to tie up a small pig and take it with us in the plane?"

Bennie thought about that one! Then he replied, "It is only an hour and twenty minutes to Manaus, and we don't have a lot of fuel weight. I suppose if the pig is tied up we can put it in the back near the suitcases and it will make it okay!"

So the men removed one of the rear seats to enlarge the space and lugged the trussed-up wild pig to the back in the baggage compartment. Looking at the animal, Bennie did not consider that wild pig all that small.

Bennie, the doctor, and the nurse clambered aboard. The engine roared in response to full throttle, and they started down the river on the takeoff run. The early afternoon wind coming from the east had raised good-sized waves that bounced the plane from one wave to another before it gained speed enough to fly. While they pounded along in this necessary phase of takeoff, Mr. Wild Pig did not appreciate the noise and the jouncing. He twisted, turned, and kicked until he loosened one of the nooses. The rest of the ropes fell off. With his long black bristles raised, the pig tottered around the nurse's seat and dashed to the front of the cabin, the loose rope trailing behind him.

As Bennie was concentrating on clearing the tree obstacles in flight, he felt something rub his right leg. He looked down. The wild pig was sinking his teeth into the edge of the cushion on which Bennie sat, and his round snout was nosing Bennie's thigh.

"Whatever happens, first fly the airplane! Keep in control!" Bennie's instrument instructor had drilled this advice into Bennie's head.

So he flew the plane in spite of the wild pig's rampage. The nurse was screaming. The Indian youngster was yelling. The doctor seated by Bennie's side swung around and somehow grabbed the beast and got its head shoved under a seat. Then he placed the seaplane's short paddle on the animal's neck and positioned a heavy foot on it, pinning the pig to the floor where it snorted, grunted, and thrashed its objections to being immobilized.

Dear Lord, Bennie silently prayed, *help the good doctor hold on to that pig!*

About a month later, it was time to return to the same tribe with their booster shots. The son of the Indian chief had received special treatment and therapy for his snakebite wound in Manaus and returned with Bennie and the medical team to his tribe. Upon arrival the youngster was the first one off the float of the airplane and raced to his smiling parents!

"Pastor Bennie," Dr. Irineu exclaimed, "we made vital and necessary points in taking their son to Manaus."

After the excitement of the young boy's arrival settled, the doctor and nurse went on with their work. A few hours later, dressed in his white medical suit, Dr. Irineu approached Bennie again.

"Pastor Bennie," the doctor said, "I know we had a rough time getting that first wild pig tied and under control inside the plane. However, the chief has again given me the best kind of a present they offer friends. He has given me another pig. I will now have a pair of pigs for my backyard. Could it be possible that we could tie him up on the outside of the plane and fly him back to Manaus?"

Bennie stared at the wild pig, the ropes, the struts, the spreader bar, and the straining rods of the floats of the aircraft and figured such a thing could be done. So they roped the pig to the struts on one of the pontoons.

After a routine takeoff and climb, Bennie had to compensate for the weight of the pig on the left pontoon. But every so often Bennie would feel something drumming on the airplane. Finally he glanced down. Lashed to the top of the float, Mr. Wild Pig II was forcefully protesting with kicks and indignant snorts as he twisted and turned in the wind.

About twenty minutes later, Bennie felt further thumps and squeals. He looked at the pontoon where the pig was tied.

The pig was gone! The rope wrapped around the strut of the plane was tightly drawn over the top of the float. Bennie carefully banked the plane to one side and then the other. Peering down, he could see the wild pig dangling from the strut. It was hanging about ten feet below the airplane, with a noose tightened around his belly just ahead of his rear hams. The wild pig, flying backward through the air with its nose behind it, was still able to breathe.

Bennie's first reaction was to land the plane. Then he thought, *I am still able to fly even if some extra right rudder is needed to compensate drag on one side. If I land way out here, something could go wrong. I better land in Manaus close to civilization, a beach, boats, or whatever.*

Bennie overflew his caretaker's house near the floating hangar to catch his attention. The man looked up and saw something small and black wigwagging on a rope a few feet beneath the airplane. After a careful splashdown and normal landing near the hangar, Bennie skied up to the seaplane's wooden ramp. Mr. Wild Pig II, dragged tail first through the wash of the pontoon, was kicking and thrashing on the rope, snorting and blowing bubbles.

What an adventure for that pig! He had been flying and snorkeling on the same day.

"Now, Dr. Irineu," Bennie smiled, as he got into his vehicle to return home and the good doctor opened the trunk of his car for his pig, "I don't think we can bring back any more wild pigs—inside or outside the airplane—to Manaus."

The doctor understood.

This is one of the United Pentecostal Church of Brazil's boats that was used for evangelizing the Amazon.

For years, this pastor made hardwood boats.

His Eye Is on the ... er, Floatplane

Established churches were growing and new ones were sprouting like mushrooms, especially in the West Amazon state of Brazil near the Colombian and Peruvian borders. Bandits and drug traffickers roamed the area, and savage Indians who had rare contacts with civilization lurked in the jungle in the headwaters of these western rivers.

Nevertheless, the search for oil, minerals, and medicinal plants penetrated the jungle. In the market of downtown Manaus, dozens of plants, vines, leaves, bark, and wood that natives use as their "drugstore" originate in the jungle. The native Brazilians boil many of these into a tea and drink it, because some of the concoctions have a long list of proven qualities for health.

Having aviation fuel spread around in drums at several churches upriver with native pastors or other trusted evangelical groups tremendously boosted the use of the seaplane. The extra fuel carefully stored in trusted hands permitted long flights and Bennie's working among churches in remote areas. Even in the dry season when local towns had used their regular gasoline or diesel, Bennie flew in with ease to splash down and refuel when river levels were so low that larger freight boats and barges canceled their trips and waited for the rains.

When any onlooker suspected evil about any operation and Bennie could not prove the truth of his latest or original departure point, he brought out the daily newspaper! He had learned to purchase two or three newspapers for the plane. In the boonies, a newspaper of the same day proved that he had flown from Manaus.

One experience reminded Bennie of the danger of flying in a drug-trafficking area. Bennie had fuel at another evangelical mission that had two seaplanes in the border town of Benjamin Constante, beside Peru and across the river from the southern tip of Colombia. Their mission personnel kindly received Bennie's few drums of fuel to hold for his use when working in the area. They locked the fuel in a room inside a floating hangar on the river's edge with their drums all kept under the eye of their church watchman.

One rainy, stormy night, a boat filled with armed men pulled up to the floating hangar and demanded the watchman to unlock this room. Drug runners always have ways and means of getting their stuff flown out, but at that time there were no legal aviation fuel stocks at airports in the Peru, Colombia, and Brazil triangle, where the three countries meet. The bandits rolled all the barrels of fuel into their boat and roared away. That costly, high-octane, light-green liquid would run drug-running operations just as it would fly planes loaded with evangelists to preach a revival.

Things could get rough if someone miscalculated or a pilot was flying in the area and not in radio communication or radar contact. In the high temperatures and humidity, any part of the electronic equipment could malfunction. The pilot was allowed to continue flying until he could land the plane, but he had to repair the equipment before he could resume his flight. Knowing this, Bennie did his best to keep his aircraft registration and all legal paperwork up to date and verified through the Civil Aviation of Brazil's online system.

God kept His eye on the little floatplane in many types of situations. Sometimes His protection prevented trouble from savage Indians. Once, a group filming in one of these dangerous border areas asked Bennie to drop into a river where such a tribe of Indians was located.

"We passed through there by boat previously and left behind an outboard motor," the leader explained. "Would you retrieve it for us?"

Not wanting to waste any fuel, Bennie quickly came in overhead, splashed down on the river, and taxied to the riverbank. Standing on the pontoon, Bennie peered through the low bushes and searched for the delinquent motor. Shock rippled through him as he spied three brawny, naked men with high bows pulled back, staring at him, their arrows aimed in his direction.

Startled but keeping his wits, Bennie smiled nervously and reached into his right shirt pocket. He gingerly pulled out a caramel—he always kept a snack on board during long flights—and with another smile unwrapped it and slowly put it into his mouth. Then he picked out three or four more candies and tossed them onto the bank.

A small boy appeared from behind the three men and, seeing the caramels fall on the bank and likely realizing the white man ate something good, darted to snatch them up. The arrows the men were pointing in Bennie's direction slowly sagged, and smiles appeared when Bennie offered more candy. After some sign language and a tense wait on Bennie's part, the Indians trudged over the riverbank with the outboard motor. Bennie did not stay too long! But he has wondered about those few caramels ever since!

As he roared full throttle over the same river the next day, the counterweights of the crankshaft popped loose. The motor sounded like an air hammer breaking up a sidewalk. Bennie coasted to a stop mid-river. The current carried him downstream, but a small boat heeded the wave of his white handkerchief and towed him to the floating hangar in Benjamin Constante. The Cessna 206 seaplane spent forty days there before a new engine was airfreighted to Manaus and placed on a boat with a mechanic to exchange it. Bennie still wonders what may have happened the day before if he'd had to remain with his "caramel friends" until someone rescued him. He recalls a friend who accepted work with the Indian foundation among the tribes on that same river. He fell to Indian arrows on this tributary of the Javarí River where today, just above its headwaters on the Juruá River in the town of Ipixuna, a fine church and a Bible school flourish.

Bennie has seen fuel injectors become plugged, magnetos fail, exhaust pipes crack, spark plugs go bad, push rods bend, cylinder head covers puncture, vacuum pumps break their axles, and the top of a cylinder on two occasions crack all the way around and come off—all during flight. For example, Bennie and his passenger, the general coordinator for the indigenous people in a huge part of northern Brazil, were leveled at 3,500 feet over the jungle, flying from the concrete bridge on BR-174 highway at the Alalau River in Brazil's most northern state of Roraima. The cooler air felt great, and the men sat back to enjoy the cruise over the tropical rain forest. Suddenly, loud, pounding thuds threatened to shake the aircraft apart. Bennie quickly turned the plane to the left and cut back on power. The green jungle below offered no opening. Reducing power to avoid the pounding of the engine, Bennie couldn't maintain their altitude, and the plane was descending at an alarming rate.

If we reach the distant river for landing, will we be over rocky rapids or a long pool? Bennie wondered. The next sixteen minutes were some of the longest of his life. He was descending with just enough power to keep the plane from being rattled apart and still reach the Alalau River. In what seemed an eternity, the little Cessna 172 finally stuttered over this river at four hundred feet of altitude. Bennie turned toward an open stretch of water, throttled back to idle—and the engine quit. The little bird coasted to a landing in the middle of the river. With the chirping of the tropical jungle birds as musical accompaniment, Bennie paddled downriver a turn or two, came to a concrete bridge, and tied up under it in the shade. Of all places to lose an engine when flying out of Manaus, he could not have handpicked a better spot for a problem to develop.

Within twenty minutes a fuel truck from Boa Vista, Roraima state, going to Manaus stopped and took the men aboard. Bennie spent that evening reading the service manual and preparing his toolboxes. Early the next morning, Bennie and a local pastor loaded the mission pickup truck with a crated new engine that Bennie had stored in his garage. After driving two hundred miles through the jungle, the men spied the concrete bridge. They backed the pickup right up to the nose of the seaplane. Then they dropped a chain through a drain hole in the concrete bridge above, and, using a hand cable jack, traded the engines' places.

"After three days of work below the bridge in shade and out of the rain, I considered it God's special, cool working place for us to exchange an engine," DeMerchant declares. "We were very near the equator."

At another time, while soaring above the Rio Negro, Bennie smelled something like rubber burning. He checked the engine compartment the next day and found that a bracket holding a fuel line covered with braided stainless steel wire had loosened and dropped onto the alternator pulley. The edge of the pulley worked slowly like an emery, rasping the metal shielding the outside of the line and about halfway through the rubber. When Bennie lifted the fuel line aside, it broke and fuel ran from the ruptured line onto the alternator, where just one spark from its brushes could have ruined his day!

Engine troubles aren't always the origin of a problem in flight. Birds can be a hazard. Once a flock of parrots burst from a tree like a cloud, and some inevitably struck the airplane. Bennie was half an hour from water to land on, so he kept on flying. In a while he smelled something that resembled roast turkey. After landing, he pulled a dead and partially burned parrot off the rear back cylinder, where it had struck in the engine compartment's air entrance against the hot cylinder and started to cook.

In a different incident after a loaded takeoff and a short climb from Aleixo Lake on the east side of Manaus, Bennie was about an hour into the flight when he noticed that the oil temperature was nearing the red line of 245 degrees Fahrenheit.

Whew, he thought. *Oil that hot would fry French fries fast!*

The sizzling temperature seemed so impossible that Bennie suspected the temperature indicator to be defective. Instinctively he cut power and circled in a descending U-turn back to the water to check it out. A bird had packed mud for its nest into the air tube that funnels air to the oil radiator and blocked off entrance of sufficient air. Bennie dug out the mud, took off again, and was relieved to see the temperature return to normal.

Sometimes danger crawls out of the river ...

Bennie landed on the Juruá River in front of the town of Caitaú. The current of the eddy pushed him the wrong way and behind a ball of floating grass, so he decided to just throttle the plane over the grass to the open water on the other side. When he opened the door, he noticed that a snake from the grass had wrapped itself around the spreader bar and a straining rod. Bennie ducked back into the plane, already in the open water, and started a high-speed takeoff water run and then stopped abruptly. The water surged over the pontoons and peeled the snake off. When Bennie reopened the door, the freeloading reptile had slithered away.

... or paddles on top of the river ...

"Just to be safe, please don't move your canoe until the plane is in the air," Bennie cautioned the members of a household he was leaving. The narrow river in front of the home had a shallow S-turn to the left and back to the right. Considering the wind, Bennie intended to taxi to the end of the S, turn the plane, and take off coming back toward the house. Cypress trees hung over the tall banks. As Bennie rounded the turn at full throttle, a canoe paddled by a young man shot into the middle of the river. To miss this canoe to the right or left would have put Bennie at high speed into the looming riverbank and probably capsized the canoe. A quick glance at his airspeed indicator showed him he was about on liftoff speed. With a quick addition of flaps and a fast yank on the stick, the plane sat back on its tail and leaped into the air a few feet over the paddler's head. As Bennie analyzed the near decapitation, he started shaking. Thank the Lord the plane was equipped for short takeoff and landing!

... or lurks on the riverbanks ...

In shoals on takeoff, Bennie has seen alligators' snouts quickly flip behind a yard away as the plane lifted into the air. On a trip to the south once with another pastor, the night came on them in the jungle. Being a clear night, the men decided to sleep on the sand. Occasionally, they flicked the flashlight beam around the beach. The ray of light illuminated pairs of red eyes from alligators that shared the area with the two men. In a similar circumstance, the taxi light from the aircraft wing revealed about twenty-five pairs of red eyes sharing the same overnight point where Bennie tied up the plane.

... or appears in the hangar ...

It is not unusual in the night when no one is present for a snake to come up a cowl flap opening and "enjoy" the heat radiating from the engine. On two occasions Bennie went to the floating hangar and discovered that a snake had curled itself on top of the horizontal cylinders of the engine behind the propeller of the Cessna 206 floatplane.

Once when Bennie arrived for an early morning flight, a snake stuck its head out and tasted the air with its tongue. "Get ready!" Bennie shouted to his night watchman. Bennie touched the starter. The whirling propeller caught and pitched the snake to the opposite side of the hangar, where the watchman killed it. So far he has found no snakes in the airplane's cabin, but Bennie keeps the doors closed!

... appears on the parts, fuel, and tool room shelves of the hangar ...

Bennie stacked some canvas beds on a shelf in the hangar room. Two weeks later when he opened the door to this dark enclosure and started to move the top bed, a *surucucu*, or bushmaster, stirred from his sleep and lifted his head a foot from Bennie's face. Bennie ducked below the shelf, spun around, doubled over, and ran back out the door screaming. Others with clubs and sticks finally killed the reptile. The only thing to which Bennie can attribute the snake's not striking him was that his hand's moving the bed left the partially coiled snake off balance and gave Bennie time to get away. Years later, when thinking of that close-up view of a bushmaster, Bennie's pulse still races!

... and even lurks in the plane ...

A passenger placed a live turtle in a bag among his stuff in the cabin of the plane. When on approach to land on the water in a narrow cove, Bennie pressed his foot on the left rudder to start the turn. Both rudders were frozen in central position.

Fearing to descend with this critical part of the controls ineffective, Bennie added power and climbed to a safe altitude to search for the cause. The rudder pedals would still not move.

"Would you slide your seat back?" Bennie asked the passenger on the right.

The turtle had crawled on the floor out of the head of the bag to the rudder pedals on the copilot's side and tightly wedged himself against them. His big rounded shell jammed the rudder pedals, locking them in position. A bit angered and with some exertion, Bennie hauled the turtle backward and threw it into the baggage compartment. The rudder controls, free of the turtle's constricting shell, responded normally.

Bennie was flying low over the approach end of the Eduardo Gomes Airport when an ant bit his ankle. Bennie reached down, found the offending insect, and squeezed it with his fingers. His head and shoulders dropping forward changed the center of gravity of the plane in flight and caused it to lose the little altitude he had over the waves of the river. Had he looked up a second later, the plane would have hit the water at a high speed and at best flipped over. Proverbs 6:6 tells us to consider the trails of the ants and be wise. The "trail" of that ant could have been written in an accident report by the Aeronautical Board. "Watch and pray" is appropriate instruction to the pilot.

Pilots have been known to go down in the high jungle and were unable to drop below the huge treetops because they did not have a long rope on board. Some have gone down under the treetops and have been attacked by jaguars in the areas where these animals have little fear of man. Anything can happen out in the boonies, so Bennie flies well prepared with tools and small basic parts. His theory is to do his best and with care and prayer depend on God to help in the rest.

Bennie was out in those wilds, getting ready to tie the Cessna 172 to the bank for the night at the Abonari River, when two uniformed military personnel who were inspecting the roadwork approached him.

"Pastor Bennie, we have a very urgent need to be in Manaus tonight. Is it possible that you get us there?"

The sun was about to set. It would be a 125-mile trip in a straight line; however, to get out of the short, narrow, river he dared not add more than a 200-mile fuel range. Bennie worked feverishly in the few remaining minutes of twilight, and at the glow of sunset they climbed through the slit of an opening through the trees. Darkness fell, and before long heavy rain pounded the aircraft. There was no turning back to the small river, but the Rio Negro was forty-five degrees to the right. With an extra twenty-five miles of flying, Bennie could make it for landing on the large body of water safely at night. The plane rocked and rolled through the rainstorm. Bennie nervously eyed his watch for timing to head to the nearest stretch of water, but the weather cleared and Bennie was able to pilot the plane straight to Manaus. He landed with his fuel reserves at a heart-catching low.

As the two passengers climbed from the plane, one man grabbed the other's hand and shook it.

"I won the bet. We will get to the big soccer game tonight!" he exclaimed.

The details of the harrowing, nerve-wracking flight through the storm in the dark on almost nonexistent fuel rolled through Bennie's mind like a reel of film.

This is just one more reason I hate soccer, he thought.

The eye of the Lord is not only on that little sparrow of a floatplane. Once He sat in the copilot's seat! Tired and worn out flying solo on a seemingly interminable flight from Eirunepé over the jungle, Bennie dozed off. The last sliver of light he remembers seeing was the needle on sixty degrees. In this "other world" of dream or vision, Bennie recognized a middle-aged captain dressed in a four-bar uniform of an airline captain. He sat to Bennie's right in the copilot's seat and looked straight ahead. Startled, Bennie quickly snapped out of his doze. He turned to the right to stare at an empty copilot's seat! In spite of Bennie's doze, the wings were level and the directional gyroscope still pointed its needle to sixty degrees!

"I am the pilot of your life," the Lord had reminded Bennie after the fearful plane wreck that claimed Sister Margaret and Jose's lives. This time He had ridden with Bennie as copilot. That experience bolstered Bennie with tremendous confidence through the turbulence he faced in later years as he led the Brazilian national church through difficult times.

The Church Explodes with Growth

Flashback to the earliest attempts at holding church services in Manaus: In mid October of 1967, Theresa with her jovial smile plied her accordion during the song service through the swirling dust and breath-snatching heat. They had sung and worshiped with a group of about eight adults. In that Sunday service Bennie was preaching to this small group that had been laboriously won to God, but who were not hearing him much of the time because of the racket of a soccer game being played in the stadium at the bottom of the hill.

After each goal a horrendous war cry went up for the favored team. This roar, reinforced by street people, amplified by a radio next door, and punctuated by a thousand fireworks, filled the sky with sound and smoke. Dogs on the loose nearby, surprised by this insult to their eardrums, broke out in a dead run as the long whoop of Goooooooooooooooooooooooooooooal trailed them. That thundering din means—goal!

At the end of his sermon, Bennie was totally frustrated. From within he heard a small satanic voice sneer, "You might as well as close your Bible and pack up your bags and move back to Canada. You will never have a church in this city!"

Wow! What a blast from the furnace of hell!

In a flash Bennie remembered how God called him and Theresa into His work on the Amazon, the special missions service he attended at Perth, New Brunswick, Canada, in 1957, and the lighthouses on the map after the crash landing on Route 13 in 1962.

In his spirit, Bennie yelled a cry he wanted the Accuser and all hell to hear: *"Satan, you are a LIAR! God called us here. There will be an Amazonian Church here! I plan to stay in Manaus if it takes my hide off—and you can put this in your pipe and smoke it!"*

Little did he know as they despondently left that service that his congregation of eight one day would be eight thousand in Manaus alone, and thousands more spread throughout the whole Amazon.

Fast-forward to the 1980s.

As the DeMerchants worked, sought God for direction, trained workers, and helped with boats and seaplanes to plant churches out on the rivers, the churches in the city also grew until years later they could no longer hold general meetings for a convention or Holy Ghost rally without searching out a suitable auditorium to accommodate the quickly growing crowd. By the mid 1980s the group in Manaus had grown to four thousand or more for larger events. The God who met Bennie in the night after the plane crash had kept His word. Life, though not always understood through its twists and turns, still held a purpose rich with promise.

One night in a tremendous service in a rented auditorium, over 350 people received the Holy Ghost. Like a flash, it dawned on Bennie! He told this huge congregation about the soccer game challenge at the beginning of the work at least fifteen years earlier at Santo Antonio's old wooden church, now relocated to a larger lot and enlarged three or four times. He told them of what the enemy spoke to him at a time of great frustration.

"I am so glad I did not pack up and leave. The Rio Negro Athletic Club was one of the teams playing that night. Tonight, years later, we are all seeing a great revival and move of His Spirit right here in the Rio Negro Athletic Club Auditorium.

"It is time tonight that we all have some Pentecostal soccer! I am going to count to three and on three we are going to give the Lord Jesus a great GOAL! We will say 'Gloria a Deus' and hold the vowel as long as you can until it is heard through these ventilated wall tiles three blocks away! Ready?"

"One, two, THREE!" Bennie's arm dropped! With it came a resounding war whoop of the great congregation full of the joy of the Holy Ghost:

"Gloooooooooooooooooooooooooooooooooo ooria a Deus!"

"Again! Louder!"

"GLOOOOOOOOOOOOOOOOOOOOOOOOO OOOIA a DEUS!"

Through the faith, prayers, giving and by the

help of the church, the team with Jesus as its coach and captain always wins. And it was with the help of pastors from the Manaus church and other established works that such explosive growth occurred.

Brazilian pastors and workers-in-training volunteered their time and effort to evangelize over the weekend if Bennie could drop them off at local churches in new areas and pick them up on return. They would sign up with the home mission department leader for a long weekend in a remote area or town difficult to reach quickly by boat. The Cessna 206 with its much greater load capacity and increased speed was a tremendous boon to the work. Bennie, with his fuel supplies for return flight stored in strategic places along the rivers, was able to lower the weight of fuel and increase the passenger load. Bennie called these excursions "Evangelistic Caravans."

These evangelistic caravans would go out on a Wednesday and preach or teach with host pastors in their cities and towns along the river and other waterways. Then it was full throttle, the roar of the engine, and the plane would hop river turns, lakes, or jungle to the next city to drop off the next evangelist. The load kept getting lighter and lighter until at the end of the line Bennie remained and ministered there. Then he would bring the workers back on the following Monday or Tuesday.

In two or three planned trips it was possible to place five passengers in the 206 in one, two, or three loads and leave them five days to evangelize in a town. The men in the bigger cities got to see and minister up close with those in other towns and rural areas and the experience benefited both. When Bennie would return to pick up the evangelist, he would tally up the people who came to God the first time in repentance during their services as well as those who were baptized in water and received the Holy Ghost.

Bennie was taking off and landing all over the Amazon, sometimes twenty-five times a day. He filled up pilot logbooks so fast, that entries of date, aircraft ID, departure, destination, and hours and minutes of flight blurred in his memory. One weekend, Bennie had nineteen different revivals going on in nineteen places at the same time!

With churches sprouting so quickly, Bennie faced the problem of having only four hands—his and Theresa's—to provide more effective administration, delegation, and sub delegation. Training others and putting them to work became the only viable option for moving ahead. One did not baptize a new convert and declare him an ordained pastor in a day, but with training, character development, and internship, ministers could often be ordained after two years.

The 1980s brought a change to the DeMerchants' family. Bennie drove Theresa and seventeen-year-old Beth to the airport in Manaus in August 1982 to leave the home nest to attend ABI in Saint Paul, Minnesota. After all the hugs, kisses, and final waves, they watched from the top of the airport observatory deck as her jet taxied between the blue runway lights with the steady red and green wing tip lights on the left and right. Bennie and Theresa held hands as they heard the roar of the jet's turbines rev up to full throttle. Then the plane flashed by in a roar and rose up to grab the night sky. The flashing red rotating beacon on top of its tail was all they could see as it became a pin prick of light and finally disappeared.

God, go with her. She is in your hands was the cry of their hearts as they choked down the lumps in their throats.

The tough parting was repeated again in early September 1987 when Pamela also left alone. The family had discussed it all together. At sometime in life the kids have to be on their own and at ABI they were going into a semi-controlled environment and would receive great training. With the girls both gone, Jo tagged along with Bennie more and more. The youngster had received the Holy Ghost when he was eight years old and was baptized in Jesus' name in the baptismal tank at the central church near the DeMerchant home in Manaus.

Jo was so serious about things of God and one day hoped to have the biggest church in São Paulo, Brazil. At twelve years of age he could sit on three pillows with his dad in the Cessna 172 during school holidays and take off and land if the wind were light with his "tutor" dad in the copilot's seat advising every move until he had nailed it down. He would fly hours cruising along rivers while Bennie read from magazines or his Bible for the next church service in these tiresome trips of a week or ten days flying by day, refueling and reaching a different town at night. Their hammocks hung close together in homes of church people in towns up and down the Amazon.

The end of the 1980s also brought a change to the DeMerchants' ministry.

"Brother Bennie, I'd like for you to oversee the work of the national church here in Brazil," Brother Robert Norris said. "I'd like to see your name as a candidate for that position."

"Oh, no!" Bennie protested. "I am seeing the hand of God in the Amazon Basin. We have a good operation going with trained men and all are working with us. We are seeing church after church open in cities, towns, villages and rural areas. Taking on more responsibility than I can handle right now would only spread me too thin and run up high administrative expenses."

It was April 1989, in Rio de Janeiro at the national meeting of the district superintendents of the United Pentecostal Churches in Brazil. Brother Norris had taken on the supervision of all of the UPCI churches in South America, but his daughter Judy had come down with a terminal disease and they had to leave for the United States.

After continuing to talk with Brother Norris, Bennie decided to present in private prayer the problem to the Lord. "Lord, if the vote for me is unanimous, I will try to do my best."

When it came time to vote in the meeting, Bennie wrote someone else's name on his ballot. Immediately he felt a strong rebuff in his spirit that he knew was from the Lord: *You are the one who is blocking My will!* So Bennie scratched that name off and wrote down his own. He was voting for himself to assume something he did not want to do!

When the vote was counted, Bennie had been chosen by 100 percent of the voters. Though pushed into a position of leading the national churches in Brazil, Bennie's primary goal remained: To plant the church that believes in one God, in only one Mediator between Him and all men on earth, that only by baptism in His name can sins be canceled, and that His infilling of each believer with His Holy Spirit is evidenced by the speaking in other tongues. And the DeMerchants wanted to realize such churches in the capital of each state, each major city, large town, small town, village, rural farm—and to every last Indian in the sparsely populated jungles of Brazil.

Having seen what was happening in northern Brazil and even in Manaus pleased the DeMerchants. They never dreamed that challenged and trained people could do what they were doing. They visited church after church for which neither they nor any of their friends had purchased a single nail to erect the building. They saw tremendous natural growth result when churches prayed, reached out to others, and through organized efforts helped send workers or their own missionaries

In one fellowship meeting Bennie asked for a showing of hands of ministers who had a church in Manaus that he had never visited. To his dismay he watched seventeen men raise their hands. Some claimed that they had been waiting in vain for him to step inside their church door. He apologized and promised to do better if they would forgive him, but until then: "You all keep on coming to our conferences and crusades in Manaus and I will see you there!"

One day, Bennie located one of these churches in an unusual yet humorous way. Bennie tells the story with a chuckle: "A pastor had purchased a roof at a good price for his church at a local hardware. He knew I had an old pick up truck with a bed long enough to put the aluminum on and deliver it. He also knew I ate lunch at home about noon. He caught me at home and asked if I could deliver the roofing to a distant suburb of the city. Of course I wanted to show my willing spirit to help his church. I followed his instructions while driving as we followed main roads and streets zigzagging to the final lot and raised building that he, as the proud guide, showed me all the accomplishments of his local church to that point."

After the men unloaded the roofing from the truck, Bennie started the drive home. At that time, he had lived in Manaus over three decades and the city had grown from a population of one hundred eighty thousand to about two million and was still expanding. The newer suburbs in these areas needed to be evangelized but to Bennie they were off his well-beaten path of years of travel to airplane hangar, the main airport, and other older and larger churches.

As Bennie drove back from this new suburb, he could not remember by what "sign-less" streets and roads he had come. He was way out in the boonies, and a glance at the fuel level of the pick up truck added to his anxiety. It was almost on empty! Lost in the northern sector of the city, he stopped to ask directions three or four times, but only became more confused.

At the top of a hill he looked ahead and spied a building with a rainbow-shaped sign. As he got closer, it came into focus and he read: "Igreja Pentecostal Unida do Brasil" (UPC of Brazil) written above its door. He grinned widely as he exclaimed "Lord, I am lost in this city's suburbs in front of one of our churches!"

Then he remembered those early days when he and Theresa studied Portuguese and had devotions alone in their small, hot apartment with Beth crawling around on the floor under the table. They prayed many times in the early morning darkness lying flat on the floor, "Lord, give us workers until they run out of our ears!"

Now, twenty-five years later, the evangelistic caravans were exploding the work in all directions.

Into Deep Waters

It happened abruptly in January 1991. Fourteen-year-old Bennie Jo complained of a pain in his upper arm.

"Jo, I know you love to do push-ups, but stop doing them for a while," Theresa advised him. "Maybe that will help your arm."

Jo was well built, tall, and broad-shouldered like Theresa's brothers. His blonde hair and honey-colored eyes made him stand out among his dark, little Brazilian friends.

"Theresa, take him to a Brazilian clinic," Bennie insisted.

After the X-rays, the doctor called Theresa in alone.

"Mrs. DeMerchant," the doctor said, "it looks like bone cancer. If you have any way to take him back to his home country, Canada, do so immediately!"

A hasty call to UPCI headquarters instantly obtained permission for Theresa and Jo to leave Brazil. For some time Theresa had felt impressed to pack her suitcase because she would be leaving very quickly, but she did not know why. Now she had only four hours to get their plane tickets, pack for the two of them, and, not believing the local doctor, plan to be back in Brazil soon. Jo was no help at all in the packing. He skipped around the house and gathered up just some schoolbooks and games.

Three weeks after a biopsy, the results indicated Ewing's sarcoma, a virulent cancer.

"Jo has an 80 percent chance of survival," the oncologist assured Theresa.

But Theresa, wanting more information, checked out books at the library. The news was devastating: Ewing's sarcoma victims had a less than 50 percent survival rate. Theresa called Bennie at the Brazilian national conference. "Ben, we are in deep water!"

Jo's faith never wavered through the routine of chemotherapy and radiation on his arm from January until June 1991. Then they heard that Brother Anthony Mangun and Brother Billy Cole would be at the Pentecostal campground in Maine at Pea Cove, not too far from Saint John, New Brunswick.

"Please, Mom, can we go to the camp?" Jo begged. "We can go back to the hospital on Monday for the next chemotherapy."

In the first service, Jo went right to the front of the prayer line for healing by the God who could do anything. Sure enough, Jo claimed his healing.

His limp arm became strong, and he could swing it in every direction.

Theresa could not deny his exuberant testimony. "I'm healed, Mom! I am not going back to that hospital!" She could not convince Jo to keep his appointment at the hospital, so they drove 250 miles back to Perth-Andover.

Tuesday the oncologist called Theresa to come at once to the hospital. Theresa explained that Jo refused chemotherapy because he felt fine, but the doctor insisted they return to the hospital.

"Mrs. DeMerchant, Jo is only fourteen. Since he is a minor, you will have to sign for him."

"My husband will be returning from Brazil at the end of July," Theresa said.

"Then we will waive the chemotherapy until the end of the month," the oncologist agreed, "but I want to see you both as soon as he arrives."

On that day marked, the three DeMerchants again faced the oncologist.

"It is against the law to stop chemotherapy," she insisted. "Your son could be taken from you and put into the custody of another family."

The DeMerchants signed papers that the hospital would not be responsible since Jo insisted he was healed. Their local social officer in Perth-Andover told Theresa that it was the law, but he would take no legal action.

A month later the three started their deputation in Ontario. There they received notice that the Saint John oncologist had taken action and they were to appear in court the next day.

They were 1,400 miles away! They made arrangements for their lawyer to represent them in court and report to the court that the DeMerchants would do whatever the court decreed. What to do and even where to live temporarily were questions that only God could solve in leading them through this experience.

A week later they arrived in Oshawa, Ontario. Brother Barrett Church, an old friend of Bible school days and also battling cancer, invited them to stay in the church apartment and seek medical help at the Sick Kids Hospital in Toronto.

"I will force no treatment," the new oncologist said, "but the cancer has spread to Jo's chest. Chances for his survival have dropped to 5 percent."

Jo agreed to go on with an experimental treatment, which was much more vigorous and debilitating. Soon his heart could no longer take the treatment, and chemotherapy was stopped.

One morning Jo, who prayed much and read the Bible, awoke and said, "Mom, I had a dream last night, but I don't know if I should tell you because it may make you feel sad."

"Please tell me," Theresa responded.

"I dreamed I was kneeling and kissing streets of gold!"

"Just because you have a dream about heaven does not mean that you are going to die," Theresa answered. She read verses of faith to him every day. He repeated them with her and had her make signs with Scripture passages about faith and decorate the room with them. Everyone who visited with him was first invited to pray.

Jo said, "Maybe I have to suffer like this so I can go to a faraway place as a missionary and suffer for Jesus!"

Prayer that circled the globe arose heavenward for Jo. Missionaries, other ministers, and visitors prayed. The Bible school in Oshawa fasted and prayed. Pastors calling long-distance prayed for Jo on the phone.

Theresa later wrote, "I always yearned for more time to pray all I wanted, but this was a year and a half of almost constant prayer!"

More severe bone pain came and more radiation. Morphine dripped in Jo's veins to alleviate the agony.

Bennie continued on deputation but told Jo, "When you want me to stop, I will." He flew in every third weekend to be with his son.

Everyone believed that at some point Jo would be healed completely. To do otherwise was to not have faith.

The time for Bennie to stop deputation had come. Jo was paralyzed except for his right arm that God had healed. In the beginning of this disease he could not move the arm for pain, but God had touched it and Jo could still hold a glass of water or write! The teenager's faith amazed the doctors as he joked with them when they examined him, and he kidded them about dying.

One day, Jo asked his doctor, "How much more time do I have?"

"Next year you won't be here," the oncologist replied.

"But I have God," the teen answered.

In the hall, the doctor in tears told Theresa that Jo was dying.

Theresa slipped into Jo's room. "Jo, pray after me, 'Lord, I belong to You. My life is in Your hands. Do whatever Your will is with my life.'"

He repeated the prayer, but every day he expected a miracle that he would be perfectly whole.

"Mom, will you read me this book about prayer?"

Theresa read a chapter that explained how to make out a check and ask for a specific thing.

"Mom, make out a check for me!" Jo pled. "I want to leave the hospital this week!"

She did so, writing the date of June 14, 1992, on the check. She filled in his name: "Bennie Jonas DeMerchant with Complete Healing from Head to Toe," and signed it "In Jesus' Name."

Jo had had his spinal column burned almost ten minutes to alleviate pain. The skin on his back resembled a big pan of raw hamburger meat. He was totally paralyzed except for his right arm. He could then hardly open his mouth to speak.

Bennie spent the night in a bed beside Jo's. Oftentimes the boy asked, "Dad, are you still there?" and Bennie would tighten his hand in Jo's and softly state, "I am right here by your side." Then he would help to change Jo's position.

Early the next morning after Bennie had dozed off, a victorious shout from Jo awakened him.

"Dad! Dad! I'm healed! I am healed from head to toe!"

From the bed beside him, Bennie responded, "Jo, raise your hands and thank Jesus!"

Jo responded, "Oh, no, Dad, I am still in the hospital. I can only raise my right hand."

Bennie and Theresa could only believe that Jo was dying and saw the perfect body he was about to enter: *For we know that if our earthly house of this tabernacle were dissolved, we have a building of God, an house not made with hands, eternal in the heavens* (II Corinthians 5:1).

Jo's vision helped Theresa to understand that as soon as we leave this earthly body, we step right into our celestial one!

It was Monday, June 15, 1992. Bennie buzzed Theresa in her room. She ran about four blocks.

"I felt like angels were whispering in my ears," she testified. "I was thanking the Lord. Something wonderful had happened. I arrived at Jo's hospital room. My husband stepped out."

"Theresa, Jo was speaking in tongues and … then he was gone."

Theresa could feel no sadness. She stepped into the room, and Jo's eyes were looking toward heaven. She gently closed them and thanked the Lord again, whispering, "I know Jo's eyes have seen God."

A brokenhearted Bennie said, "The Lord giveth and the Lord taketh away." All his dreams for his only son had been shattered.

God gave Theresa super power and grace through it all. Bennie was at a loss as to where to start funeral arrangements. But just seconds after Jo passed from this life, the phone rang. It was Brother Rooks from Miami. He said that he had tried all over to find the DeMerchants early that morning.

"What's up, friend?" he inquired.

Brother Rooks gave them the phone numbers of Brother Judd, the foreign missions secretary, and other numbers to call for immediate help. Bennie's cousins, the Melvin DeMerchant family, came quickly to help them move out of the room at the hospital in Toronto. Friends in Oshawa helped them move out of the church apartment the same day. Pamela arrived from college in Saint Paul, and they drove twelve hours the next day to Perth-Andover, where their relatives and friends provided more support.

Thank God for the church! Brother DeMerchant's old home church, Calvary UPC in Perth-Andover, donated a burial plot in their cemetery after a huge funeral with relatives, friends, and forty-four ministers present. Pastors Harry Lewis and Dana McKillop officiated at the memorial service on June 18.

Shortly after Jo's death, Bennie was asked to preach in the Plaster Rock church, where as a teenager he received the baptism of the Holy Ghost. The loss of their son did not alter in any way the DeMerchants' faith in God. In prayer he tried to think of a subject that would be the Lord's will and the best for that service. So many things unreeled through Bennie's mind in hindsight over Bennie Jo and his situation. *If we had only done this or that, maybe it all would have been different*, he thought, but finally he concluded that all their steps had been ordered by God and that He knew the way through the wilderness that included all the merry-go-round of clinics, hospitals, treatments, doctors, nurses, drugs, and living on wheels or wings. He and Theresa came to understand that BJ, as they and others had called him at times, was a loan to them, and all that happened would result in God's glory and divine will and should never alter their faith to believe in healing.

"Lord, what do You want me to preach?" he cried.

The unexpected topic rocked him.

Dad, that was fun to land a salmon!

"Hotel" accommodations in far-flung churches

A floating church building was towed
to start a UPC church.

A Charge for Theresa

"Preach on healing!" There was no mistaking the positive directive.

So just three days after Jo's death, Bennie stepped into the pulpit at the Plaster Rock church and poured out his heart.

"God heals," Bennie declared. "God works miracles. Whether He healed our son or not does not lessen His divine capacity to stretch forth His hand and heal."

As he continued ministering, the Spirit focused biblical examples, experiences of some Brazilians, and personal experience into sharp clarity. The words flowed with faith and power. Bennie wanted the whole world to know that nothing would stop or slow their walk with God nor kill their faith in His great will and plan or their call to continue His work in Brazil.

The DeMerchants were able to recuperate in the following weeks and in August 1992 returned to their home in Manaus for their sixth missionary term. They were now "empty nesters."

Theresa had spent most of her life raising three children on the mission field and working with the ladies, the choirs, and other functions in the local church a couple of blocks away near downtown Manaus. While Bennie flew up and down the rivers in his seaplanes planting churches, Theresa took care of the office, shopping, banking, and driving the children half an hour each way to a Missionary Society English school in west Manaus. Before the advent of computers simplified her work, she laboriously made up PIM bimonthly letters by hand and mailed them from Brazil to each donor using information and pictures Bennie supplied.

In 1990 the national Bible school in Rio de Janeiro closed for over three years to recover from debts and to reorganize. There was no Bible school or hope that one would soon be opened in Rio. During this closed period, the youth who desired to attend Bible school approached their pastors in Manaus and the outlying rural churches and asked about going to school. These pastors met regularly in Manaus to solve the problem. With or without Rio, the local ministers decided that they would start a Bible school in Manaus.

Shortly after their return to Brazil following BJ's death and mostly out of curiosity, the DeMerchants attended this meeting to observe their solution. The pastors wanted to have their own Apostolic Bible Institute (ABI) in Manaus. With sacrificial labor donated by the ministers as teachers, the men reasoned that a Bible school could operate in the central church. The location was perfect: near the DeMerchants' home and only two blocks from the central bus terminal in the city where all buses of the suburbs of the city converged.

The men decided that the Bible school would operate on Monday, Wednesday, and Friday for three hours per night for nine months. After two years, a student would graduate with over six hundred hours of classroom time. The ministers agreed that the local churches in Manaus would not hold services on these three Bible school nights. The teachers would be those who had graduated from the Rio Bible school and were active ministers. Each pastor would donate one night per week to teach the youth. Other rules and guidelines would be established.

Then the ministers startled Theresa. They elected her to coordinate this operation! And Bennie and Theresa had attended the meeting only as observers.

In time the curriculum, based on the Alpha courses of the international church, was established. Some valuable subjects the DeMerchants had studied at ABI in Saint Paul, Minnesota, were inserted into the program. The most basic subjects were taught in the first year.

Theresa submerged herself into meeting the challenges of organizing a Bible school. In January 1993, six months after Jo's death, the ABI in Manaus started with about a hundred students. The classes budded and then blossomed, even though the downtown church, built in 1969, was small, hot, and noisy. Second-year students had classes on a small balcony without student desks. Everyone soon felt the strain of the cramped quarters.

Bennie talked to the Lord about it. "Lord, we need a larger place. We need big bucks to build a Bible school on the lot behind our church that our people purchased by a long struggle. We need a large, two-story, air-conditioned Bible school building that will accommodate up to three hundred students. The building can also be used for ministers' meetings or assistance in crises for our people. We need at least five classrooms and an administration room."

Bennie actually had someone draw up the plans. When he looked at the cost to build the envisioned school and considered their operational deficit growing monthly, his heart sank! Only God could supply the need! Only God! But like Hezekiah laying Sennacherib's letter before the Lord, Bennie spread out the plans for the building.

"Only You can do this, God!" he insisted.

On January 12, 1994, Bennie was munching his lunch when he received a phone call by SSB radio patch.

"Pastor Bennie, your American friend who is fishing had a stroke. He's about three and a half hours' flying time away above the equator. He's unconscious and needs immediate removal from the head of the small Tapará River in the jungle."

Bennie took off solo from Manaus two hours later with plenty of fuel for a seven-hour round-trip. When he reached the camp spot, the fishing group's manager and chief guides helped carry out an unconscious Tom Nash in a hammock to the plane. They laid the seat back and tried to make the man comfortable. With just a glow on the distant horizon,

Bennie climbed at full throttle through the clearing between the trees. Though the sick man did not respond, Bennie reassured him that the flight would be okay as they flew south.

He calculated his touchdown time and radioed Theresa to meet them at the Manacapuru ferry crossing on the shore of the Rio Negro in the São Raimundo suburb in west Manaus. She drove the fisherman to the hospital before midnight and stayed until she knew the man was in intensive care.

After putting the airplane into the hangar, Bennie returned to the hospital in Manaus and spent some time with the fisherman. Then he phoned for the man's medical records from the United States and took them to the doctors the next day.

In the evening of January 14, a medical jet arrived in Manaus from the USA with doctors and the sick fisherman's anxious wife on board. Bennie accompanied them to the small hospital, where soon preparations were made to remove him to the States.

In spite of all efforts to save the fisherman's life, he died two days later. Bennie, saddened by the man's death, was comforted by his attempt to save the man's life.

Months later the Foreign Missions Department informed Bennie that a foundation the man headed had sent a check to be deposited to Bennie's account. Bennie turned from the telephone, a strange expression on his face.

"Bennie!" Theresa caught her husband's expression. "What has happened? Why do you have that look on your face?"

The Apostolic Bible Institute trains thousands
of youth for ministry in Brazil.

Manaquiri church and Bible school

Mayday! Mayday! Mayday!

"Remember that fisherman who suffered a stroke a while back? The one who died in spite of all the effort to save his life?" Bennie asked his wife.

"The one for whom I met you at Manacapuru ferry and drove to the hospital?" Theresa remembered that night very well!

"His foundation just sent a check for one hundred thousand dollars to our missions account in the States," Bennie said, his expression changing from one of incredulity to jubilation. The money would go toward building a quarter-million-dollar Bible school that would accommodate three hundred ABI students.

Theresa, with an empty nest, turned her considerable organizational and supervisory skills to the development of the Bible school, securing teachers and coordinating their schedules, developing curriculum, and copying and distributing materials. Bennie, of course, continued his missions-by-air program.

One evening he reminded Theresa that he planned to rise early and fly into the Hiscariano Indian tribe on Mapueira River, a two-hour flight over the rising jungle highlands northeast of Manaus.

"Pack plenty of those good salmon and mayonnaise sandwiches," he suggested.

During the night Bennie dreamed that he was strolling through the door of an approved aircraft engine overhaul shop. Wandering among the engines mounted on stands in the room, he neared one that he recognized to be the same type as the one in his airplane. He stopped to investigate the engine's exposed internal parts. In his dream, he turned sideways to look more closely. It seemed that he was peering through a huge magnifying glass that revealed a very small, fine crack in a connecting rod of one of the engine's six pistons.

He jerked awake. Then realizing he had been dreaming, he went back to sleep.

As Theresa prepared Bennie's breakfast and packed a lunch for him the next morning, Bennie, remembering the dream, decided to change his flight plan and visit Coari, a city 235 miles west. Except for a loop of the river to the south about halfway, the flight would put him over water about 80 percent of the time. If he made this trip with no incident, that weird dream of a defective internal engine part was just one of those tricks the mind plays on a person.

"Theresa, I'm going to Coari today instead," he remarked. "I'll make the trip over the jungle after I get back."

"Why did you change your plans?" Theresa asked.

Bennie chose not to answer her question. Although visual and instrument charts filled his side pockets, he rarely opened them since GPS with modern satellite navigation all but made them obsolete. Mentally he reviewed the route he had flown many times, visualizing the church in every town he would pass over. Coari had eight churches and a Bible school—and drums of fuel for flying beyond or returning.

Bennie, accompanied by two men from FUNAI, gassed up the Cessna 206 floatplane two hours later at the floating hangar in east Manaus. They took off and climbed along the Amazon River, flying west. Air Traffic Control received their flight plan from the VHF radio as Bennie rapidly recited the ten items the controller needed. They would check out of his Terminal Control Area (TCA) on time.

A few minutes after passing Manacapuru, they reached this point, so Bennie keyed the microphone and reported that Papa Tango, Lima Echo Echo, was vertical of the TCA limit. He reported their estimated time of arrival (ETA) in Coari. PT-LEE is the airplane's national federal registration for Brazil.

The controller answered through Bennie's headphones, "Have a good flight."

A low overcast was burning off and rising, so Bennie leveled off at only 2,500 feet. Until then he had flown along the Amazon River, but after flying an hour, Bennie spied the river looping to the south after passing Anori, where they had a church. Twenty-five minutes ahead, the river would swing north, where Bennie would intercept it at Coadajás, the location of three churches and a Bible school.

As Bennie passed Anori, the engine purred and all engine instruments—oil pressure, oil temperature, cylinder head temp, exhaust temp, and others—registered in the green. The plane left the mighty Amazon to cut across the green jungle to save fuel. This neck of land contained an extensive swamp with lakes too small to land on except for one large lake ahead which years earlier Bennie had decided to use as a stepping-stone emergency stop if he ever needed it. Bennie trimmed the plane for level flight and reached for the bag of sandwiches. He handed one to each of the other men. With a quick prayer of thanks, the men bit into their sandwich snack. The "stepping-stone" lake swung halfway past the plane's left wing. The thin line of water of the river curving back to the route lay ahead. Below, a woman washed clothes at the riverbank, soaping them by hand. She heard the throb of a distant plane engine and glanced up.

Then suddenly the engine sounded like the rattling of a dozen automatic guns at the same time—and then fell silent. To the three on board, the sound reminded the men of a jackhammer breaking up a sidewalk. Smoke and black oil poured out of the engine compartment as the propeller wound down to a stop in the air.

Bennie pulled the mixture and switch, turned the fuel selector to off, and threw the master electrical switch as the plane coasted down from the clouds.

They were gliding with no power. Bennie could see the Amazon River ahead beyond the jungle below.

If I can coax the plane to that river, we will not be in an abandoned rain forest lake, he thought. *People will have boats and be going up and down the river, and we can soon get out by boat and tow our airplane to repair.*

The heavily loaded plane refused to be coaxed into anything. It lost altitude fast.

The black, alligator- and piranha-infested lake, though behind them, was closer than the river ahead. Bennie banked the plane and aimed it toward the lake. After clearing the trees, he dropped the flaps and scored on the water with a mild squash. The plane water-skied over gentle waves in the breeze and coasted to a stop.

With sighs of relief, the men exited the plane and stood on the pontoons. Bennie breathed a prayer of thanks that they were all safe. His Global Position System marker read 03.49 S and 61.51 W. Had he flown his original flight plan from the day before, they would have gone down over solid jungle and probably would never have been found. Such a fate had happened to many others.

The engine had indeed exploded in the air. The central middle left cylinder had been blown off the block and through the engine cover over it, leaving a nine-inch-wide hole in the motor's casing. Bennie grimly examined the plane and the shreds of the factory-built engine.

Bennie thought and prayed, *God, the day this Humpty Dumpty is put together again with a*

*new engine and I go full throttle with this
aluminum bird on this lake, You will be one great
big God!*

The sun shone brightly overhead. Black oil
laced with rainbow colors traced their arrival over
the last hundred yards of water. They floated safely
and serenely in the wind. And that was the problem:
the serenity. Hunters or fishermen used the
abandoned lake only seasonally.

*We might be here a long time before we are
spotted*, Bennie thought.

Trees standing in the tea-black water
surrounded the lake entirely. With the paddle from
the plane, the men could maneuver their floating
bird, but with a thirty-nine-foot wingspan, how could
they paddle among the trees? Floating islands dotted
the crescent-shaped lake. The trees lining the water's
edge offered no hint of a break that indicated a trail.

"Let's check out the shoreline," someone said.
But they may have been paddling a barge, so
unwieldy was the plane in the wind. Finally, sweat
dripping from noses and chins and turning their
clothes into movement-hindering bandages, the men
spotted the makings of an old lean-to. They tied up
there to explore it but discovered that its floor was
barely above water level.

"If we have to spend a rainy night here, that
shabby, rotten thatch will offer no more protection
than a sieve," one of the men observed.

So after the wind dropped off, the men just
paddled their "winged boat" around the edges of the
lake, checking for any sign of higher land and a
possible trail going south toward the Amazon.

Finally, a lift to the land on their right gave them some hope. They aimed the plane that direction.

One man stepped over a low mound, hoping there might be a path or some connection to dry land. He returned in just a few minutes. "I saw a huge alligator with a snout the length of my arm," he exclaimed. "I don't think we are going to walk out of this place!"

Fortunately, the plane was equipped with a VHF radio that would transmit and receive almost in line of sight with slight refraction. Checking on an instrument chart for aircraft radio frequencies, Bennie picked the one in bold black letters indicating the high-altitude frequency jet planes would use for their position over that area. Bennie switched to that frequency at on and off intervals to spare the battery. But for the farthest reception and transmission, he had to be in the middle of the lake to avoid the trees that would block any communication.

About four hours after downing the plane, Bennie turned on the radio again and listened. Hallelujah! He heard a jet captain reporting his high-altitude position to Manaus Center as he flew to Brasilia.

Bennie firmly and calmly cut into his transmission.

"Mayday! Mayday! Mayday! Papa Tango Lima Echo Echo!" As his heart thudded in his chest, Bennie repeated his mayday call twice more. He wanted that pilot to know who was in the Amazon jungle!

Would he answer? Bennie sweated into his headphones. He knew the little battery would not last long even with reasonable use. And then Bennie heard the pilot utter those magic words: "Manaus Center, stand by. I have an emergency caller! Good day, Lima Echo Echo; go ahead with your message!"

This was no time for small talk. Bennie tersely reported his actual GPS position. Any pilot with these eight numbers and two letters in hand could fly straight to them from anywhere.

"03 degrees 49 minutes Sierra, 61 degrees 51 minutes Whiskey!" Bennie slowly repeated the numbers three times for the pilot, who copied that location and iterated it.

"We are three men down uninjured in emergency landing in a Cessna 206 seaplane on a swampy lake in middle of jungle 110 miles west of Manaus with engine severely damaged. When you arrive to next airport call my wife collect and advise her of my position so she can send my other floatplane here to get us out. We are okay. Do not activate search-and-rescue operations unless delayed." Then Bennie recited his phone number.

The pilot copied Bennie's information and read it all back. "Have a great day!" the pilot said.

Yeah. Sure.

The men were glad that Theresa had made lots of sandwiches! They could ration those; the problem was that in the heat they would soon use up their good water supply, and drinking the lake water could give them amebic dysentery. They spent a long night trying to sleep in the Cessna seats while swatting mosquitoes. Toward morning a storm broke over them, and the deluge pouring off the wings provided them with fresh drinking water.

Early the next morning the trio maneuvered the plane to a low, narrow islet where an abandoned open-sided, thatch-roofed shack on stilts rose about a meter above the ground. Two small shelves revealed some hay wire and salt. A swamped dugout canoe lolled in the water. During the day they could hang hammocks and rest sheltered from the blazing sun.

Bennie had no fishing equipment with him, but on finding some pieces of leftover salted fish, he curled one end of a section of the hay wire around a piece of the fish and dropped his improvised fishing line into the water. Piranhas from nearby floating grass swarmed and swirled, and as they hit the long piece of baited hay wire, he jerked them over the low side of the dugout canoe. After some time, he had thirty-five small ones in the boat.

With a fire and salt, we could have three men eating man-eating fish in case we are not able to get out of this place soon, he thought.

In the early afternoon of the second day, the trio heard the welcome sound of a turbo-prop passenger plane of Taba Airlines that at that time of day flew between Manaus and Tefe. Bennie decided to back up his message with the second plane as long as the battery still held power.

Bennie knew the radio frequency the Taba pilot operated on, so he radioed him. When the Taba pilot realized the plight of the three men, he immediately turned in their direction. Bennie could hear him approaching their small shack and on the radio advised him he was coming louder and louder.

Finally the pilot answered, "Oh, yes, I see you behind the trees on the lake."

"Can you tell me how far it is to the Amazon River south and if there is any dry land?" Bennie asked. The helpful pilot, an acquaintance of Bennie's, flew further south and at the Amazon River circled back. "No, Pastor Bennie," he replied, "it is all swamp, at least twelve miles of it. Stick with your airplane. Someone will come."

What amazing help! This regional airline in flight had broken off to follow Bennie's call and, even with a planeload of passengers, had descended to investigate the situation!

The messages did get through. The first airline pilot did call Theresa. Lincoln, a young commercial pilot whom years earlier Bennie had taught and encouraged to fly, was on the way with the Cessna 172.

Late in the afternoon of the second day, the men heard the distant putter of an airplane propeller. Bennie recognized the sound of his Cessna 172. He could not control his emotions! Hot tears streamed down his cheeks as he said to himself, *DeMerchant, you are crazy. You are crying like a little kid!* Minutes later the men looked up as the pilot, Lincoln, circled and landed on the water, taxied up, cut power, and stepped out on the pontoon with a paddle.

"Pastor Bennie, your name is all over the airport pilots' talk in Manaus. If I do not get you out today, a helicopter will be in here tomorrow."

When he inspected the damaged plane and shattered engine, Bennie's pilot friend just shook his head. "This is unbelievable! I've never seen anything like this!" he said.

(The hole that was formed by the cylinder when it blew off the block later required 108 rivets in the cowling sheet-metal patch that covered the engine. Seeing these flush, sanded, and painted-over rivets reminds Bennie of the dream. When the mechanic told him where the engine had apparently broken, tears streamed down his face.

"It was what God had shown me in the dream," he says, his voice choking with emotion.)

Before dark all the men were quickly jumped out to Anori to a local hotel, where they ate and slept well. Two trips in the 172 returned them safely to Manaus.

On subsequent trips to Coari for church services, Bennie would drop down and check on the 206. A month later, a new engine was air-freighted to Manaus and loaded onto one of the mission's church boats.

A group from the Manacapuru church, using their twelve-ton, covered church boat, toiled for half a day with power saws to claw through the jungle to get to the 206 to exchange engines. Then accessories were hooked up and tested on ground runup and break-in.

On January 20, 1993, Bennie and his mechanic, Francisco, taxied the 206 on this black, tea-colored lake. The smell of new, heated engine paint filled the cabin. *Lord, You spared my life with a dream. I now have a new engine. Here we go again!* Bennie thought as he lined up into the wind. The engine sounded great—new and tight. With a long, steady pull, the men eased out of the half-moon lake and climbed in a slow circle, gaining enough altitude to reach the Amazon River.

It was full throttle one more time, with a new engine ... for about an hour.

Distributing New Testaments

Large new church in Lábrea under construction

Miracle in a Cow Pasture

Deep in the bush on Murumuru Lake between Anori and Coadajás, Bennie and his mechanic, Francisco, had installed a new engine in the 206, immobile for sixty-three days. Now on its maiden voyage, the new engine had checked out perfectly before takeoff. While the 206 seaplane cruised above the Amazon River fifteen miles west of Manacapuru in the early morning of February 20, 1993, moderate rain beat on the windshield. In the lowering weather conditions, Bennie was following his IFR rule of I Follow the River.

Then at an altitude of about 1,200 feet, the engine stuttered—and quit.

No big deal.

Tanks run dry in flight and in a couple of seconds, with hardly any loss of speed or altitude, the engine will resurge when fuel hits its injectors from the other wing tank, Bennie thought.

But the tank that Bennie had switched from still indicated almost half full. Automatically, he switched to the opposite wing tank and pressed the auxiliary fuel pump switch. The propeller wound down in the wind as the engine lost RPM. It gave a quick surge and died again. It was unbelievable, but it would not restart!

Heading the plane east, Bennie saw the Amazon to the right when the engine quit, but in the time it took him to switch fuel tanks, the plane lost three hundred feet of precious altitude. Waves on the water indicated a strong wind change from the south. At first the river seemed within gliding range, but almost immediately Bennie had second thoughts. The strong wind was right over the nose, and the plane, heavily laden with parts, toolboxes, leftover mineral water, food, and bedding, sank rapidly. Bennie tried to choke down a big lump in his throat when at three hundred feet altitude above the trees he realized that, at such a rate of descent, he could not reach the river.

How quickly his heart rate changed! He craned his neck for an alternative place to set down—now! Near the river's edge beyond the trees a small cow pasture—minus cows—appeared.

This plane is not a chicken that loves land! It's a duck! Look for water! What other alternates do I have for a dead-engine landing? Bennie wondered.

In the rain and downdrafts, the plane's glide rate seemed not much better than that of a grand piano! Mammoth samauama trees clawed the sky above their lower forest friends. There was enough lumber in one limb of one of these enormous trees to build a wooden house. They were the first to meet the level of the wing tips as the plane silently coasted downward, its three-bladed propeller motionless. When Bennie saw the tops of these trees go by level with the wings, he realized how low they were. He stretched his neck to see where the plane was going and prayed repeatedly and earnestly, "Only You, Jesus! Only You!"

Still flying, Bennie glanced out the side window. Looking up, he saw the tops of these huge trees at least fifty feet above the wing tips. Thoughts flashed! *Am I flying blind between trees in this rain? What next?*

Bennie braced himself to feel and hear the pounding of ripping metal any second as the outstretched tree limbs reached for the plane's pontoons. Holding his breath, he held the plane in a slight sideslip for forward visibility as the plane's nose rose and speed dropped off. While looking out the side window, he suddenly spotted the end of that minuscule cow pasture. The quickly sinking plane was over it! As he extended the flaps fully, wet bushes shook as they brushed the Cessna's pontoons. With its nose up, the plane squashed down and rumbled like a double wagon going too fast over a rough sidewalk. Pontoons dug into the wet grass and mud, spewing water sideways.

At any second Bennie expected to crash into a tree stump or hidden log in the grass, left there by the Amazon hand farmers to burn or rot. He held the stick all the way back while the plane grabbed the ground, lurched forward, and tried to nose over in a somersault, but miraculously it scooted on the wet grass and came to an abrupt stop, still upright!

"Wow!" Bennie exclaimed to Francisco, whose hand was under his on the fuel selector switch. "I have made rougher landings on the waves!"

They were loaded almost to gross weight and had landed "dead stick" in this small cow pasture without cartwheeling! The rain beat on the windshield and the inside steamed as final prayers of gratitude filled their hearts.

"What's damaged?" Bennie asked when he caught his breath.

"Check it out," Francisco said.

Bennie opened the door and dropped to the left float. Francisco slid across the pilot's seat and jumped down behind Bennie.

Ignoring the rain, the two men searched in vain to find a bent, broken, or cracked float strut, fitting, or straining rod. The bottom of the pontoons and sides were normal. All was intact. The floatplane just sat there proudly with its pontoon keels on the wet grass as if an angel with a hydraulic lift had picked it up in the warehouse and daintily set it down, right there!

Two keel marks scored the mud and grass. Curious, Bennie traced them in the rain to their starting point. He stared at the lofty trees that he had just glided between on an emergency landing approach in drumming rain. He studied the steep approach angle the plane had taken. The only exact spot where the pontoons could safely touch in that incline was at the end of the handkerchief-sized jungle cow pasture!

Pacing the pontoons' skid marks back on the grass, Bennie found that the plane initially touched down in a small mud puddle about fifty to sixty feet wide and about a foot deep in its center. Two rows of grass in the puddle lay parted from its midpoint. Noting the freshly riled water in the center of the puddle, Bennie waded out to check its depth. The deepest part lapped at his leg just below the knee. It was exactly where the plane made first contact with the surface of Mother Earth.

Bennie and Francisco looked all around and only then realized the extent of the miraculous landing. That little, knee-deep puddle was the only puddle in that sloping field. It had provided a slippery ski action on impact that allowed the plane to slide upright as it surfed to a stop.

"God, You have got to be great and this machine mighty tough!" Bennie rejoiced. "Only You, Lord! Only You! I could not put that plane in the middle of that puddle again under these conditions if You allowed me a hundred tries!"

Dogs from the house about a hundred feet to the left started to bark. Someone opened the wooden back window of the building and looked out into the rain. A small child in his mother's arms peered through the window of the house and started to cry. A big bird with two huge, white bananas under it had silently arrived from the sky and landed in their backyard. Two rain-soaked men pranced joyously around it and acted so deliriously happy that they seemed drunk. Below a steep riverbank a hundred yards beyond the floatplane, the mighty Amazon flowed silently eastward.

257

Why did that engine stop in flight?

All had checked out the night before, but rain had poured most of the previous night. In addition, the plane had been waiting in the lake sixty-three days in the middle of the rainy season before this new engine was installed. Upon investigation, the men discovered that hardened rubber "O" rings had allowed water to seep into the fuel tanks.

New or old, no aircraft engine in all the world will burn rainwater!

Now only one question remained, and Francisco asked it.

"Pastor Bennie, how do we get a floatplane on pontoons out of a cow pasture?"

High and dry after dead engine landing!

The Greatest God
of All!

"It's not going to be a problem to get the plane out of this cow pasture," Bennie assured Francisco. "But it will take a lot of hard work."

The river flowed nearby, thirty vertical feet below the field. But slightly downhill several hundred feet away, on the other side of two barbed wire fences, a larger pond half smothered by floating grass offered a potential watery runway. After the rain stopped, the two men unloaded the heavy cargo and five passenger seats, drained the water from the fuel, and siphoned all but thirty minutes of the remaining fuel into jerry jugs to lighten the aircraft. The farmer obligingly lowered sections of his fences. With skillful use of their machetes, the natives scythed away the grass to transform the pond into a water run.

About fifty onlookers gathered, and for three hours many of them helped cut arm-sized saplings they then laid in front of the plane. After draining a couple of glasses of water out of the plane's fuel system, Bennie started this new engine and grinned as it purred smoothly. Then, with three hundred horsepower pulling hard up front, they pushed and coaxed the unharmed Cessna, steering it by the tail when necessary and skidding it across the saplings for fifty to sixty feet. Then they switched the saplings from behind the plane and laid them in front of it again. After repeating this procedure several times, they crossed the field in a direction parallel to the river and nosed the plane into the pond.

With some trepidation, Bennie took off. When jubilantly airborne, he circled back to squash down on the river, where his helpful new friends lowered the cargo, the seats, and the jerry jugs into the plane. Bennie and Francisco refueled the aircraft and returned to Manaus without further incident.

A few years later Bennie was rolling some full barrels of aviation fuel from the ground into his pickup truck when he felt some strange, needlelike pains in his chest. After he rested a minute, the pains subsided and he continued his normal day. He mentioned this later to Theresa, who broke into his busy schedule with an office call to a cardiologist friend in Manaus.

"Go to have that checked out!" Theresa insisted.

After giving Bennie a few tests, the doctor surprised him. "Pastor Bennie, you might have at least two coronary arteries plugged."

"What medicine would resolve the problem?" Bennie wanted to know.

The doctor promptly answered, "Bypass surgery!"

"When does this surgery need to be done?" Bennie asked, thinking about visitors from America who were arriving shortly for some very good seminars. Bennie was also committed to a conference in the south.

The doctor's adamant response was "Immediately!"

Bennie advised the cardiologist of his own "immediate" plans and that such a surgery, "if necessary," be done afterward.

The cardiologist made no rebuttal but simply phoned Theresa. Theresa, ever competent, arranged for their flight to Miami and packed their suitcases.

Bennie's liberty for the next few days was stolen, and from then on he would have to be obedient to the international medical authorities sent with an executive jet with one mission: airlift the flying missionary out of Brazil on June 18, 1999. Bennie was strapped onto a stretcher and watched a heart monitor screen as the plane taxied to the active runway, already cleared for immediate takeoff. As the small, powerful jet gained speed, Bennie watched the white bars speed by and felt the plane become airborne. "God, bring me back into this place one more time to continue our mission in Brazil!" he prayed.

Bennie had open-heart surgery with five bypasses. After three days in ICU and three more days in the hospital, Bennie was released from Mount Sinai Hospital on June 29, 1999.

In the long days and nights of recuperation, Bennie prayed and thanked God for His great gift of life. God drew very close. Bennie dared to challenge Him: "God, You will be a much bigger God the day my passport is stamped back into Brazil!"

After Bennie's uneventful recuperation period in Canada, that day arrived when, in the early morning of August 6, a Lloyd Bolivian Airlines airbus crossed the equator and reduced power for the long descent to Manaus. Later DeMerchant's passport was stamped to allow him to reenter Brazil. He felt strong and well. His great God had instantly become his greater God!

But as thankful as he was to be back to Brazil, Bennie had one more deal to propose to God. In prayer he laid this proposal before the King of all the earth and with whom we will reign forever and ever if we are faithful to the end.

"Lord Jesus," he prayed several times, "the day my medical certificate for flying purposes is restored and legal, You will become the greatest God!"

Weeks later Bennie's cardiologist carefully examined and questioned him about many things and checked lab reports.

"You are okay," the doctor said. "Your exams show you have recovered normally from your surgery and are a lesser risk for flying than previously. Keep in touch with me. I will watch you."

Then the doctor filled out a form that Bennie would need to take to the aeronautical medical air force clinic for recertification for active pilots. On the form the doctor wrote: "I see no reason why the applicant cannot continue to perform his aeronautical duties." Then he dated, stamped, and signed the document.

When Bennie returned home that day, he laid this document on the middle of his bed, bowed in prayer, and, weeping in joy and humility, declared, "Jesus, once again You have shown Yourself to be the greatest God of all!"

A lovely UPC in Cruzeiro do Sul, Brazil

ABI graduates Maurice and Fernanda serve
in Portugal.

The Cezar Moraes family from Brazil was sent to
Mozambique as missionaries.

The Fishhook Church

Bennie was flying low along the Autazes River in the year of 2002 when on his right he saw a woman below in her front garden waving a white towel. He was hurrying to get back home to one of Theresa's nice lunches and so continued 'til reaching the other side of the river. He glanced back as her small house on the riverbank receded in the distance. He was a mile away when something inside him triggered a turn back signal. That place seemed worth the risk of burning half a gallon of aviation fuel, so he circled the plane to leave her one of his aerial invitations to a UPC of Brazil church not too far away on the river where she lived.

While flying back to this waving woman, he reached into the open side pocket by his left knee, where he kept a wad of small plastic sandwich bags. Each of these little, insignificant stapled bags contained a sheet of paper folded twice. On the upper right in bold print it read: "A present for you!" in Portuguese with a # 3 long shank Mickey Finn streamer fly stapled to it. (If a peacock bass does not hit or roll for one of these flies in a few minutes, don't waste time trying something else!) Each folded sheet of paper inside stated how to catch bass and the best times and conditions for fishing. The reverse side of the page briefly described the churches, their locations in the Amazon, and the telephone numbers of about fifteen of the principal churches in Manaus.

As the woman picked up the air-dropped present, Bennie felt satisfied. Turning the plane, he roared full throttle back up to altitude and on to Manaus. The following Sunday the woman and her family chugged along for six hours in their eight-ton, covered hardwood boat with their small diesel inboard engine to the nearest church at Mount Sinai on the Autazes, where all ten of them filled an altar before the ministering pastor, and four of them received the baptism of the Holy Ghost. Marital disharmony and other problems disturbed her large family, but from then on their life improved and their home became a preaching point for other folks nearby on the river. The pastor later helped them with meetings, and they built a new church beside the family's house on the riverbank. Bennie thinks of this congregation as the "Fishhook Church."

God blessed this family to become fruit and vegetable suppliers of large quantities for the nearest town's market. Some of the profits from this business were turned into a fine white ceramic floor, an object of pride in this well-decorated church.

En route to the ever-growing number of churches in northern Brazil, while flying low and in sight of people, Bennie would occasionally flip one of these bags out the window even in the rain. If it fluttered down onto water, the air inside the thin transparent plastic kept the streamer fly floating until the fastest canoe paddler was able to grab it from the water. If someone did not see it, it would float for months or be blown by wind to the shore, the white paper standing out among the jungle shades of green bushes in water or red clay banks. Each receiver of this fishhook present could catch fish, but Bennie used these aerial invitations to fish for men. The recipients were invited to attend churches in towns and rural areas as well as in Manaus. The final statement read: "It does not matter who you are or where you live. You are our special guest and invited to attend one of hundreds of our churches in the Amazon!"

Pastors told Bennie that this trick brought people into the church from everywhere. They came in clutching the little plastic bags to try to get one more of these "red and yellow things" that will really catch peacock bass; the gospel then netted many of them!

The head of the family whose wife picked up the Mickey Finn streamer fly is now a local licensed minister. His daughter, Marciene, married a young pastor, Brother Marcelo, who was trained in the Bible school in Nova Olinda do Norte on the huge Madeira River. Using a long, slender, light aluminum canoe and engine with a long propeller shaft, Brother Marcelo oversees about five works, including the Fishhook Church. In high water and using a compass, Marcelo motors through flooded swamps and cuts off thirty miles or more of following the river because the narrow canoe can slip between and around the bushes and trees. For a few pennies, the "M and M's" can go a mile against the current and have home Bible studies and baptize families in that area.

Brother Marcelo rarely stops. Some of these lakes or islands have five hundred or more hardworking rural people, many of whom readily accept the gospel and, when trained, become good workers. Bennie has seen some of these trained workers in a year of labor raise up a solid church of a hundred members who also reach others. This domino effect of church growth would take a lifetime to do in First World countries.

For example, in an area about three hundred miles west of Manaus, the huge Piorini Lake nourishes a surprising population of Amazonians. Some trained workers out of the Coari church by boat reached one of these lakeside villages of around one hundred people about five years ago. The Pentecostal church was the only one in the village, and all attended service for which Bennie and Theresa splashed down. Theresa had some boxes of used clothes to hand to their public school teacher, who knew everyone's sizes. Piorini Lake is sparsely populated, but four other villages hug the nearby shores.

"Now we have a church in all five of these villages, and in March 2008, boats converged on Piorini Lake for a big fellowship meeting," DeMerchant states. "We expected a thousand people for services. They usually bring their bags of manioc meal and other goods from a market and kill two or three young cows and have their big, happy Oneness Pentecostal time."

A thing as insignificant as a fishhook started people toward God and proves a principle from His Word: "the weak things ... confound the things which are mighty" (I Corinthians 1:27).

Such a simple thing bringing folks into the kingdom confounded Bennie also. When he turned his life over to God to go to the mission field, in his sincerity he sold his fly rods and his fly-tying equipment. He later discovered peacock bass while stopped on a jungle bridge in his car. Upon the advice of the locals, he decided to try. Countless hours bent over textbooks trying to learn Portuguese cooled his missionary ardor for a while. Needing a break from the intense studying, he asked his brother to send him a three-piece fly rod through the mail. As he stood on floating logs in Manaus and fished the open spaces between them where these peacock bass abounded, onlookers claimed that he was "whipping the fish." They began to laugh, but after Bennie caught a few, they asked him for one of the fish for their lunch.

Bennie recognized that the Brazilians had a resource that one day, when they woke up and promoted sport fishing for bass, would half-fill airlines with rod-toting fishermen, who would often pay one thousand dollars a day to go long distances in boats to fish in places where Bennie fished for free! His Lord had taken a liking to him! Fly-fishing had a new dimension. One flew and then fished!

When sports writers for national magazines started looking for someone who had information about fishing in the area, Bennie's name came up. They tape-recorded Bennie's answers to their questions while he flew them to their destinations. Their stories were then printed (*Sports Illustrated*, May 18, 1981, "Please, Don't Fall In the Water," page 78; *Field and Stream*, December 1995, "F&S Bonus Adventure: Fishing in the Green Hell," page 59). Some of these many sport-fishing companies are multimillion-dollar operations with their own air-conditioned luxury boats containing bars and buffets; fleets of aluminum canoes; and seaplanes (*http://www.peacockbassflyfishing.com*).

Any visiting North American pastor who preached a campaign for Bennie enjoyed a trip of R&R, which, of course, included fishing. On one trip, the late Brother Nathaniel A. Urshan flew with Bennie to some nearby places for relaxation. A monkey hanging from a tree spotted a banana in Brother Urshan's canoe, dropped down, snatched it up, and jubilantly leaped back to his overhanging branch!

The two ministers had so much fun they stayed too late and had to full throttle back under the radar along the riverbank. After they landed in the dark, Brother Urshan quickly changed his clothes and with Bennie hurried back to thousands at Rio Negro Sport Club Gymnasium for another night of hard preaching in breathtaking heat.

To Bennie, there would never be any leaders greater than Brother Urshan and his fine wife, whom he heard as a small boy preach and sing at Plaster

Rock, New Brunswick, convention. The Urshans turned the Amazonians inside out with their singing and worship of our great God, the Lord Jesus Christ!

2008 update: The M and M's opened a new church on a tributary to the Autazes, the Acara Grande River, just thirty minutes flying south of Manaus. Four months after opening, the church in Acará had about forty-five to seventy folks in attendance. Its official dedication was September 8, 2007, with about two hundred attending.

Churches were started from
air-dropped streamer flies.

Ticuna Indians of upper Amazon greet arrival of
UPC Brazil plane

Pastor Marcelo in his aluminum canoe

The Jerusalem Project

Leading people has tense decision-making times. Even with the best board and representation of the larger group, few decisions in critical matters have a solution that will please all. Some problems are like the proverbial pineapple: "No matter how you give it to another, he will be pricked!"

In the Manaus ministerial conference of 1993, Bennie watched the election results as the ministers of the city voted on their next leader for the Manaus district. They chose their own Brazilian pastor, Luis Almeida dos Santos, who had been among the first converts in 1967.

"This is a historical day for me," Bennie proudly announced from the pulpit. "God called me into this work in this city," he continued, "but if you elect another in an open conference, you will relieve me of being involved in your administration and problems. It will be great to receive phone calls and give out the phone number of your new district president!"

Having doubled and grown to about 125 churches in a short time, Manaus, the capital of the huge Amazon state, again divided into an East and West Metro district. Each side met monthly with their ministers and boards in a large local church easily reached by city buses from every suburb. Together they organize for growth and solve their problems.

In 1981, Bennie needed to purchase a lot for his watchman to live near the seaplane hangar on the north side of the Amazon River. While he shopped for property, a family offered to sell him a large jungle lot at a point on the river's edge. Bennie wanted only a small lot on shore in front of the floating hangar. The family made him a deal for the bigger area in exchange for rice and bananas.

Why so cheap? The DeMerchants later discovered that a foul-mouthed witch doctor lived next door. He was always trying to pick a fight or cause harm. And it was no small task to have bushes cut every few months by hand machetes to keep the jungle and squatters out.

Since 1981, no local church building had been big enough for general meetings. They rented auditoriums, but the logistics of moving benches and plastic chairs and installing sound systems and hauling in lumber to build the platform were a daunting task. Often on the eve of such a meeting, after they had paid for the use of the building and were given a receipt, some other person or group with more jurisdiction would advise the Pentecostals that they could not let them use it as scheduled. Even when they rented facilities from other churches, these other groups decided at the last minute that they also needed the space for their own.

At the turn of the century, tired of wrestling with this problem for years, the Manaus district sought property on which to build a convention center. The board members searched all over the outskirts of the city for suitable property on which to build. Finally they approached Bennie.

"Pastor Bennie, can we use your big lot on the river to build a convention center on?"

They decided to name the undertaking "The Jerusalem Project." The lot was out of the city in the middle of the jungle east of Manaus with just a mud road curling around the top of the nearby hill. During the rains, bus access on this jungle mud road would be sloppily difficult.

"I advise against the enormous expense of erecting a building large enough to hold five thousand people," Bennie replied. "It is cheaper to rent. This construction would be extremely costly. Plans and approval, tons of steel girders, cross beams, and reinforcement steel with twenty thousand square feet of sheet metal to roof—it will take a long time to build and pay for. People lose enthusiasm when a project goes on too long. With the American dollar dropping to half its value in three years and the cost of materials rising—well, it defies completion.

"Going blindly ahead with this Jerusalem Project might be to do something without first counting the cost," Bennie continued. "It would be good for you to build a much smaller and needed prayer shed where different local churches in town could continue their all-night prayer meetings. If it rained, you would be inside."

This seems most practical economically with our limited means, Bennie thought.

But the churches in Manaus had been steeped in the power of prayer. For several years prayer bands had met for all-night prayer sessions on this huge riverfront lot. God would help them to complete this Jerusalem Project *and* supply the funds to support their missionaries abroad in other Portuguese nations *and* aid the many other needy areas of Brazil.

Bennie was surprised one Monday morning to see the Brazilians had turned their zeal into action. A church member had access to a company's large bulldozer. With their small offerings in the beginning they could hardly buy the diesel for this big machine. Bennie refused to buy so much as a tank of fuel. They were forging ahead against his advice, and he was going to watch!

From the top of the lot where he stopped his four-wheel-drive pickup and where the mud was undisturbed, he watched the bulldozer chew deeply into the side of the rising hill and level the lot at the end of the point that jutted into the meeting of two of the world's largest rivers, the Amazon and the Negro.

After a week of bulldozing, the now level lot seemed bigger. The bulldozer's lags clacking away plowed swaths of orange earth toward these two rivers. Its blade rose high and in reverse it raced backward for another push of ground. The lot was becoming a huge tabletop for a convention center whether Bennie liked it or not.

The drive of even poor people uniting to build the Jerusalem Conference Center made Bennie understand that he was no longer head and shoulders above them in economy and decision making. His huge lot was more or less confiscated by the Manaus district. He finally nodded his head and let the district have it all properly registered. The small baby of a church that God had given them, whose first offering was twenty-two American cents before he added his dollar in 1966, was now becoming adult or at least an adolescent church that could handle more tasks. This fact was driven into his brain by the action he witnessed. In a week the top of the hill was at the bottom.

Pieces of the puzzle fitted together. The incorrigible witch doctor who caused so much trouble died drunk. The government erected a huge penitentiary on top of the hill, housing hundreds of inmates, and shortly afterward paved a road to and beyond it to within a stone's throw of Jerusalem. What a blessing that mud-eliminating asphalt is!

Weeks later Bennie looked toward the two vast rivers mixing together a mile from Jerusalem as the columns were going up on this huge building. Bennie did not expect this. Truckloads of steel were arriving on the lot, and welders were putting beams and trusses together. A successful young businessman whose life was saved from drugs and marital problems was both heading the construction and traveling from church to church, asking each to give to Jerusalem. This jungle-of-steel roof overhead would withstand the direct wind coming from the east and south from the Amazon and would provide free air conditioning.

To build the basic Jerusalem Project with the needed steel was beyond their immediate means. In the dry season, the unstoppable saints were already meeting in open-air services among the columns to worship together by the rivers of Amazon where the DeMerchants (on the platform) sat and wept for joy knowing the humble roots of this church and realizing where it was going. But it was still open-air, and what steel they could buy was on the ground beside it.

Unexpectedly, God moved on people in the United States, who themselves had financial and natural disasters from hurricanes, to send sacrificial offerings to push the Jerusalem Project forward. It proved to the DeMerchants and Brazilians alike that God could provide supplementary funds from any source. They were able to contract a firm to make use of the work and materials still on the ground. A large crew quickly welded and put up the trusses and steel overlaying beams and roofed the building.

In September 2005, they had rented an auditorium for the Manaus Bible school graduation. The week before the occasion, history repeated itself.

"Your use of the building has been canceled," they were told, their prepaid receipt ignored. Again.

They had to move fast. When they announced to the churches that the graduation was to be held in Jerusalem, some really doubted it would all work out. They scrambled all week to get the lighting system in place. Dozens of buses loaded with saints from all the churches in Manaus arrived at the Manaus ABI graduation on September 24, 2005. A surprise awaited them! God had quickly answered their prayers! The huge building they had prayed for was completely covered, and long fluorescent lights hung everywhere from the high overhead steel beams. It was fully lighted!

Soon afterward, on November 12 and 13, the Jerusalem I Conference Center filled again. Hundreds of people stood in the dark on the outside also, watching as Brother David Myers of Palm Bay, Florida, a missions-minded pastor, private pilot, and friend, powerfully ministered. The Amazonian people standing in this massive group loved him. Soon the altars filled, and Pentecost happened all over again.

In 2006 Manacapuru also received a new landmark. The UPC of Brazil, under Brother José Ribamar de Lima's leadership there, built a new conference center, a general meeting place for churches in their district. Jerusalem II, seating 3,500, occupies a small city block that has to be closed to motorized traffic because at peak attendance times an additional 1,500 people stand in the surrounding streets. People arrive by bus, car, or boat to receive or be renewed in the Holy Ghost.

Jerusalem I, Jerusalem II, and all the other Jerusalem-minded churches in the Amazon are reaching out to "Judea, Samaria, and the uttermost parts" of the Portuguese-speaking world. The native saints, many of them very poor, shamed Bennie by their generous giving! In 2000, with great cost and sacrifice, they sent Brother Cezar and Sister Vilma Moraes and their three grown children to the African nation of Mozambique. In the world conference in Malaysia November 8-11, 2000, Brazil was asked to help some war refugees who returned from Malawi to Mozambique. These refugees were in contact with the Crumpackers and had started a work but needed help and direction by Portuguese-speaking missionaries who could train and organize the work. The Brazilian board in their next meeting appointed the well-qualified Moraes family, who in 2002 settled on location in Beira, Mozambique, as home base for the next five years. Supported by the Brazilian church with a vehicle and large rented apartment, the Moraes family completed their first five-year term and returned for six months for a furlough in Brazil. Their labor has resulted in a strong Mozambican church of nearly seven thousand believers and hundreds of trained ministers.

More workers have left Brazil to serve God in other Portuguese-speaking countries. Sister Alcina Lima, a retired Brazilian federal government lawyer who is very sharp in studies and teaching, moved to Portugal with her son Mauricio and his wife Fernanda to help the Portuguese UPC although it meant living off her limited retirement income. This fine Christian lady spends days on end on a computer, translating Bible school material from English to Portuguese. She researched publishers who, with the aid of UPCI Ladies' Ministries, in about one year added forty thousand textbooks to the stocks of the growing Bible schools, which have expanded to 1,100 two-year course students. The work using these new missions materials in this old, colonial country of Portugal doubled last year.

On October 12-14, 2007, Brother Brian Abernathy and Brother and Sister Lloyd Shirley blessed the Brazilian churches in the cool, open-sided Jerusalem Center at another ABI graduation. It was beautiful! About three hundred other ministers attended the services. The Brazilians presented a plaque of appreciation to the DeMerchants for their ideal for the Amazon.

Bennie, standing on the platform next to Theresa, looked at her and whispered, "How different this is from the night we arrived!"

Brother Abernathy preached powerfully the following two nights, striding up and down the long aisles while the congregation roared as he made point after point. After the ushers stacked chairs away from the platform to open a huge space, people flooded the altar.

"We all celebrated a fiftieth-year anniversary since the first missionary family appointed by the UPCI, Sam and Lois Baker, first set foot in Brazil," DeMerchant reports. "I was so glad then that of my sixty-six years of life, forty-three were spent helping to build a strong United Pentecostal church in Brazil."

As Bennie looked over the awesome congregation of thousands of Brazilians united in worship, he was reminded again of his dream when he was ten years old.

"The dream has never left me," DeMerchant states. "In the dream, I saw at my feet the meeting of these two rivers, the coffee-cream-colored Amazon and the black-coffee-colored Rio Negro that at flood time flow next to each other over one hundred miles before mixing. The Jerusalem I Conference Center is just north of this meeting point. The Jerusalem I project will, by the end of 2008, have added wings. An extension will be built on the east and west sides called 'Judea and Samaria' to accommodate the people and double the capacity of Jerusalem I."

What fulfillment of a dream—a promise!

"May the Lord Jesus help us to keep going ... full throttle!" Bennie and Theresa say.

And all the congregations reply, "Amen!"

About the Author

Delores (Dolly) McElhaney, a graduate of Apostolic Bible Institute, Macalester College, and Tennessee State University, began writing when Jesse Norris recommended her to Edna Nation, a children's editor for Word Aflame Press Sunday school literature. Subsequently, over four hundred of her stories were published. She has penned three books: *Born with a Mission*, in conjunction with Carl Adams; *Angel at My Shoulder: The Agnes Rich Story*, and *Faith Brings an Empty Basket*, coauthored with Jack Leaman. She has also worked as a freelance copy editor for Thomas Nelson Publishers. For eight years she wrote articles for *The Print Out*, a bimonthly magazine produced by the Public Relations Department of the then Nashville State Technical Institute, and edited and proofread most of the material published by that school during her employment there. She lives with her very understanding and supportive husband, Bill, and two horses in a retirement community in sight of the Great Smoky Mountains.